All Scripture references taken from the KJV of the Holy
Bible, unless otherwise indicated.

SEASONS OF SIEGE: *GOD IS COMING* by Dr.
Marlene Miles

Freshwater Press 2025

Freshwaterpress9@gmail.com

ISBN:

Paperback Version

Copyright 2025, Dr. Marlene Miles

All rights reserved. No part of this book may be reproduced,
distributed, or transmitted by any means or in any means
including photocopying, recording or other electronic or
mechanical methods without prior written permission of the
publisher except in the case of brief publications or critical
reviews.

Table of Contents

SEASONS OF SIEGE:
GOD IS COMING

COLD OPEN

It's a siege. A full-blown siege if the enemy is all around.

I've seen the Lord perform in two ways. Maybe you've seen other or different ways, but I will share how He has revealed Himself to me in seasons of enemy opposition and specifically siege for the purposes of this book. Those two choices? Either God is preparing a table before me in the presence of my enemies. Or, I am to arise and thresh because He drew the enemies for one of those two reasons. One to watch me dine in peace and comfort, in spite of them, or perhaps after they realize that God is God, I have my energy restored now I am to arise and thresh them.

When the enemy has fully surrounded a person or a city, not partial pressure, not harassment, but *encirclement,* Scripture does not leave ten options on the table. It collapses to two. Those two are not really options, they are possible outcomes, or possible methods of outcomes. Either way they have little to nothing to do with the besieged; those options are all about God.

In my life, these are two ways that I've seen God behave. However, God can do whatever He wants, and in anyway He chooses.

Either God is preparing a table in the presence of enemies; and I'm not even afraid. Or, God is drawing the enemies in so He can authorize decisive action. Else, why would anyone's enemies be either drawn or invited?

Those are the only two outcomes when the siege reaches fullness. Anything else is misdiagnosis.

You prepare a table before me, even in the presence of my enemies. This is Psalm 23, and it is not poetic comfort this is siege theology. A table is provision without effort. It is nourishment without escape. It is authority without battle, and it is dignity in confinement. A table means you are invited. You do not break ranks; there is a head of the table and often there is a head table. You do not negotiate, you do not panic. There is authority there and you do not self-rescue.

You sit, because movement would interrupt what God is doing. In Scripture, when God feeds people in siege conditions: manna falls, oil multiplies, ravens bring food. Hezekiah's pool continues to bring water to the city. There is provision and sustenance; strength is sustained supernaturally.

The enemies remain, not just any enemies, but the passage says _**my enemies**_; these are known enemies. Provision appears anyway. I have written this book not to talk about myself, but to share experiences and revelation and to help the reader who may be *going through*. Even in siege, God provides. In my house, there was coffee when I know there was no coffee in my pantry. A friend mentioned a certain brand of salt, I looked in the cabinet, I have that salt where I've run out of the other brand. In my business, I needed the copy of a key but had no time to go get it. A copy of the key was found at home on my desk, even with a tag fully labeled as to what this key goes to. (When and why did I have two keys to that same internal door in my office?) In my wallet there is money that I KNOW I didn't have.

That is provision. That is God saying: **"This one is Mine."** God in His own ways lets you know that He is there; you are not alone, even in a siege.

This book is not about predicting how God will end a siege or forcing Him to do so. It is about recognizing when the moment has arrived, how to behave until it does, and stand when it has. A siege does not mean God has lost control, although the enemy may think that. A siege means that the field has been set. The table is prepared. The floor is ready. The question is: Has God told you to sit at the table, or to arise and go to the *floor*?

INTRODUCTION

In Seasons of Siege, start out knowing that God is coming. When enemy forces surround a city, a stronghold, or even a person (one of His) cutting off essential supplies, trying to provoke surrender of their opponent, that is a siege. It is warfare. In the Bible, sieges were common. They caused significant hardship, suffering, famine and unheard-of acts by the besieged who became desperate to survive.

There are seasons when faith feels active. There are seasons when loss explains the pain. There are seasons when waiting still carries expectation. And then there is **siege**. A siege is the season where you are not doing anything wrong—so it seems, yet nothing moves. Obedience continues, you're doing the best that you can. You are doing all you know how to do, but relief seems elusive. Prayers are going up, but you wonder if the Heavens are also besieged because where are the answers to your requests to God?

This book is for people who have already prayed. Already fasted. Already believed. Already obeyed. Already endured. Already asked all the right questions of the Lord; and already did the warfare. But they still find themselves enclosed. A siege is not always a battle you fight. It is a pressure you survive without losing yourself.

In Scripture, sieges were not signs of weak faith or divine abandonment. They were periods of containment—times when movement was restricted, resources were rationed, and the people inside the walls were forced to confront a truth that could not be bypassed or hurried.

Sieges are not always loud; sometimes they are quiet. They do not tempt you to sin, they tempt you to quit, or to self-rescue, to abandon posture, do something desperate, or to surrender ground prematurely just to feel relief. This is why so many faithful people misinterpret a siege as failure. But a siege is not failure. It is not punishment. It is not just stagnation; it is a season where movement is prevented until intervention—not effort—becomes the solution. God sends the intervention, only God.

Did a million or more stand at the Red Sea, with Pharaoh's army following after them? That was a siege and their solution was by Divine plan and authority of God: keep walking.

This book will not teach you how to "break through." It will teach you how to remain intact until relief arrives. Relief? Yes, by faith, God will arise, He will come or He will send relief, even if it just a Word. Even one Word, sometimes that is all you need. God will see this through because it is **His** mission. Your job, my job is to stay obedient and fully aligned with God. A siege is not a mission of action, but a mission of trust. Nothing is required except obedience, restraint, and remaining with God.

In this book, you will learn why striving worsens a siege. Why what used to work no longer works. How to stop blaming yourself for enclosure. How to wait without withering. How sieges end in Scripture. How to recognize relief when it comes. How not to be tempted by fake or false relief that are actually traps.

Some seasons are meant to be endured. Some are meant to be fought. And some, like siege, are meant to be outlasted under divine protection until divine relief abates the siege.

Enclosure is where the walls seem to close. Options narrow--, really, are there any options anymore? Doors shut quietly; you may not be aware that they have shut, when they shut, or how long they've been closed against you. Movement becomes restricted--, you seem to be able to move, but are you going in the same old circles every day? No clear exit presents itself.

Enclosure is not opposition—it is containment.

Attrition is a strategy of war. It is when strength drains quietly. Energy decreases without drama. Hope feels rationed. Motivation wanes. Weariness replaces urgency. Attrition is how sieges work—slowly, invisibly.

Interruption is when what worked stops working. Familiar prayers feel flat. Old strategies fail. Spiritual tools lose traction. No need to go to your usual go-to's--, they don't work anymore. Even the people you used to count on, can't find them or they are saying No when they used to say yes to you. Productivity stalls. This is not loss of power—it is a shift in requirements.

Exposure: something must surface. Something has got to give. Hidden dependencies are revealed. Misplaced trust is exposed. Timing is clarified. Self-rescue impulses are confronted. Sieges end when what is hidden can no longer remain hidden.

Relief is when intervention arrives. There is a sudden shift or change. There is external movement. Pressure lifts quickly, even instantly. Authority is restored. Relief is almost never gradual; it is decisive.

WHAT IS A SPIRITUAL SIEGE

A spiritual siege is when the enemy believes he's got you. You are surrounded and blocked on all sides. When the enemy is trying to outlast you know that is a classic devil move. When you are not exactly being oppressed, harassed, tormented or bothered spiritually, you are just quietly surrounded, or you feel surrounded. The devil believes that you don't know he's there. He believes you may fall into complacency because he doesn't seem to be actively oppressing you right now.

The goal is not seduction anymore. You have peace within yourself that you know you are not doing anything sinful or wrong--, and you don't even want to. You may have previously fallen, but you got back up repented, renounced, denounced and ask for forgiveness from God and cleansed and consecrated yourself. You have asked to be covered by the Blood of Jesus. You have no sense of sin-guilt over anything right now. But somehow nothing is working. Nothing.

The enemy's goal is not confusion; you may even feel that you are thinking clearly now after having come through confusion. No, the enemy's new goal against you is exhaustion, attrition, and collapse from within. This is siege.

Prayer may feel dry. Scripture may feel flat. Commonly used spiritual weapons don't seem to be working. Progress reverses. You feel surrounded rather than attacked. You're not tempted to sin as much as tempted to **quit.** A siege says "I don't need to defeat you. I just need to wait you out."

Your previous go-to tools that *used to work* stops working. Those tools were designed for open combat, not enclosure.

A famine is lack without opposition. A siege is opposition that creates lack. In famine, provision may be scarce, but movement remains possible. In siege, provision is cut off *because access is intentionally blocked.* Famine calls for endurance, stewardship, and trust. Siege calls for discernment, restraint, and posture.

HOW YOU KNOW YOU ARE IN A SIEGE (NOT JUST A TRIAL). You are likely in a spiritual siege if several of these are true at once:

1. You've already obeyed God, yet pressure increased

2. There is no obvious sin to repent of, yet resistance remains

3. You are not even sure if your prayers are being opposed; that's what you want to think. The other temptation is to think that they are being ignored.

4. You are under attack functionally, more than emotionally. You may be asking God, "How do I live?"

5. Your strength is being drained quietly, not violently

6. You feel sealed in, hemmed in, or stalled

7. Breakthrough is not denied but unnaturally delayed.

8. What once refreshed you now barely sustains you

9. You are tempted to withdraw to conserve instead of advance

10. Hope itself feels rationed

That is siege language.

THE FIRST CRITICAL TRUTH. You do not break a siege by fighting harder. That is how people burn out, lose discernment, and turn inward. Sieges are not broken by louder prayers, More fasting, longer nights, Repeating declarations, over-spiritualizing things. Just plain exhaustion.

In Scripture, **sieges are broken by intervention, reordering, or exposure**—never by sheer stamina.

STEP ONE: STOP TRYING TO "WIN" This is counterintuitive but essential. A siege feeds on your output. The enemy wants you producing, explaining, proving, defending, wearing yourself out. The ideal may be simply enduring silently, So the first step out of a siege cease performance. Do not cease prayer; never cease faith in God. However, cease *performative effort*.

Now, you must calm yourself from all hyperactivity and as my mom would say, "Turn it all over to Jesus."

In your prayers, find out from the Lord what is going on. Lord, I sense that there is some kind of embargo going

14

on around me. Things that used to work don't anymore.... Is this You Lord? Am I under judgment? Once you find out that you are not, then find out from the Lord, what is going on? and, what do I do? How do I handle myself right now?

I sense that I am surrounded and by enemy forces, is this accurate, or ask honestly, or "am I tripping?" The Holy Spirit will answer you. If you are looking at a siege situation, then He will tell you.

Lord, deliver me from enemies that are too many for me, or that are too strong for me, in the Name of Jesus.

This aligns you with **siege-breaking authority**, not siege endurance.

STEP TWO: CHANGE YOUR POSTURE (FROM SOLDIER TO CITY)

In Scripture, individuals experience sieges the same way **cities** do. Cities under siege do not chase the enemy. Send everything outside the walls, Exhaust the inhabitants.

They close gates, ration movement, secure leadership, protect the well, wait for relief. Spiritually, this means to close unnecessary access points. Conversations that drain. Teaching when you're not replenished. Explaining your season. Over-sharing spiritual processes or experiences. There may be *monitoring spirits* present to report back everything you say.

Curse not the king, no not in thy thought; and curse not the rich in thy bedchamber: for a bird of the air shall carry the voice, and that which hath wings shall tell the matter. (Ecclesiastes 10:20)

15

STEP THREE: IDENTIFY WHAT THE SIEGE IS AFTER.

Every siege has a target. It is rarely your calling, your destiny, or your future. Those come later. A siege usually targets one of three things: Your authority – making you doubt your position. Your continuity – making you stop mid-process. Your testimony-in-progress – making you abort something unfinished. Ask this (don't rush it): "What was forming when this pressure intensified?" That is what the siege is guarding against.

STEP FOUR: ASK FOR REVELATION OVER RELIEF

Asking, "Lord, take this away." "Lord, change this." "Lord, fix this." May not be the question. Jesus, yes, Jesus asked the Lord to take away that siege that would be the Cross, but then He yielded to it. Siege-breaking moments come when people ask, "Lord, what must be exposed for this to end?"

In Scripture sieges end when supply lines are cut, when traitors are revealed, when timing shifts, or when God Himself intervenes publicly, not privately.

STEP FIVE: WAIT WITHOUT WITHERING

This is the hardest part, waiting under a siege is not passive. It is refusing despair, refusing self-blame refusing to abandon posture, refusing to force fruit. Waiting says "I trust God, putting your faith fully on Him." God does not shame people for being under siege. He relieves them.

When a siege breaks, it usually breaks suddenly, not gradually. Scripture shows sounds in the night. Enemies fleeing without explanation. Supplies appearing. Doors opening unexpectedly. Authority returning instantly. Entire bodies of water dividing so people can crossover even on dry land. This is why endurance—not panic—is critical.

This is not a "10 steps to breakthrough" book. It's a manual for people who are faithful, tired, and boxed in. We will discuss why God allows enclosure. The danger of self-rescue. How to wait without losing yourself. The difference between famine and siege. When silence is strategic. And, recognizing relief when it arrives.

This book will save you if you feel ashamed that you're tired.

This You Tube video might be helpful to you if you are really tired. It is from my Warfare Prayer Channel. https://www.youtube.com/watch?v=l3kxT8KZyzc&t=5s

THE TABLE

There are passages of Scripture that feel like relief simply by being read. Psalm 23 is one of them. *The LORD is my shepherd; I shall not want.* (Psalms 23:1). He prepares a table before me in the presence of my enemy. The passage doesn't call this a siege, but if enemies are present and you're not even afraid or concerned, instead you are dining. That is God. That is faith.

Green pastures. Still waters. Restored souls. And then comes the line that feels almost indulgent in its kindness:

"You prepare a table before me in the presence of my enemies." Most of us know exactly what that sounds like. A table suggests warmth. Care. A host who has thought ahead. It suggests safety. Even while danger exists somewhere beyond the edges, it does not touch us here. The enemies may be present, but they are not in control. They watch from a distance while we are fed.

This is not survival food; it is not food that seems rushed like the Passover meal where there may be imminent danger just outside the door. No, we are in green pastures, relaxing even; this is abundance.

When the enemy surrounds, Scripture does not leave the moment undefined. Yes, we believe that a table means comfort, rest, or passive provision. That reading is sentimental, shaped more by pastoral imagery than by Scripture itself. A table is not a restaurant, however.

Sometimes it is a place of meetings. Sometimes it's a place of negotiations. In Scripture, a table is often a place of decision, exposure, and separation.

And more often than not, it is also a threshing floor.

Psalm 23 has been softened by familiarity, but what if the table was never about eating? *"You prepare a table before me in the presence of my enemies."* We picture a peaceful meal. David, who wrote this Psalm was a warrior king, not a shepherd-poet reclining in a meadow. He protected the sheep. There was at least one lion and one bear that David had to contend with, and we certainly know of one giant that a little shepherd boy would not be able to defeat on his own, without God.

A table in the ancient world was also a place where grain was processed. It was a surface where separation occurred. It was a site of judgment and discernment, a boundary between what is kept and what is discarded. Threshing floors were flat, prepared places. They were exposed and public. They were dangerous. They were where weight came down. So, when God prepares a table in the presence of enemies, He is not offering distraction. He is declaring: *This place will decide the matter.*

Table and thresh are not opposites. We have been taught to think that a table means to rest and to Thresh means battle.

Scripture does not support that division.

A threshing floor *is* a table. A table *is* a threshing floor; a threshing floor can be like a table. Both involve separation, authority, process, permanence, and no return to the former state. What differs is not the location, but what God authorizes you to do there.

The enemy does not surround to observe. The enemy surrounds to try to force a premature decision. Surrounding pressure is meant to produce panic, negotiation, self-rescue, foolish mistakes, surrender, abandonment of assignment, But Scripture shows something else. When the enemy surrounds, God has already claimed the ground. Encirclement does not mean ownership. It means containment of the conflict. Nothing else enters. Nothing else leaves. The matter must be resolved here.

Two postures, one God--, Our God. When a siege reaches fullness, God reveals posture, not method. There are two. **1**. Sit at the Table. To sit is not to quit. It means you do not run, you do not bargain, you do not self-rescue, you can't, else you'd be trying to rescue yourself in your flesh. Or, if you are not accessing God's authority you would have to use some illegal power, and that will not only not work, it will get you into some serious trouble. Sitting at the table, you remain nourished by God, who has prepared this for you, while the enemy watches.

This is not weakness. This is God and you acknowledging your humanity; flesh must be fed. It is restraint under authority. God feeds people in sieges because movement would interfere with what He is doing.

Manna fell. Oil multiplied. Strength was sustained. The enemies stayed. Provision came anyway. This is the table.

"You anoint my head with oil; my cup runs over." Oil soothes. Oil heals. Oil honors; it authorizes. A cup that runs

20

over means there is more than enough, not just for now, but for what comes next.

In this psalm, God does not seem hurried. He is not reacting to threat. He is not scrambling to protect. He is hosting. If any man answer, *I will come in to sup with him.* (Revelations 3:20B, NKJV) The invitation is clear: sit, rest, receive.

The table tells us something deeply personal. It says, *You are known; you are seen.* Your hunger has been noticed. Your fatigue has been accounted for. Your fear has not surprised God. You are human with human needs and frailties.

The table is not generic. It is *your* table. Your enemies are not ignored, but neither are they centered or feared. God does not remove them first; He feeds you first. That alone is a comfort. It suggests that even under pressure, even when surrounded by circumstances or people that oppose you, God is not frantic. He is attentive.

Psalm 23 does not deny danger. It names it. *Though I walk through the valley of the shadow of death, I will fear no evil.* Notice the wording: *through.* Yet, the psalm does not rush to escape the valley. It lingers. It reassures. In the presence of God, the diner is not afraid or begging God for defense or deliverance; God's Presence is stronger than threat. *For You are with me.* The table is one of the ways God shows that Presence. Not by removing conflict immediately. But by sustaining you in the middle of it.

So, while we humans may be freaking out, God is preparing a table right in front of these enemies. Shall we sup? Shall we dine with the Lord?

For many, this image has been enough. Enough to breathe again. Enough to survive another day. Enough to trust that God is not absent, even if answers are delayed. That is not wrong. The table has carried people through grief, illness, injustice, and waiting. It has taught us that provision does not require escape. That Peace does not require silence. That nourishment can exist while enemies remain. This dining is consummation of covenant and relationship. Dining is intimate. God prepares the table first.

Pay attention here because in the next chapter of Psalms there is the King of Glory, strong and mighty in battle. Psalm 23 goes into Psalm 24 as a deliberate progression. Psalm 23 answers the question, *How is the righteous sustained while surrounded?* The answer: *The Lord is my shepherd... You prepare a table...* Psalm 24 answers the question that follows, *Who now has the right to enter, rule, and take the field?*

Lift up your heads, O you gates... and the King of Glory shall come in. (Psalm 24:7)

By Psalm 24, gates are addressed, doors are commanded to open. The King is announced. Questions are asked and answered. Authority is declared publicly. The shift is dramatic and intentional. You don't *feed* the King of Glory. You make way for Him. The table prepares the ground for the King.

The people have been steadied and readied. Fear has been dealt with. identity has been clarified; now the field is ready for His arrival.

"Lift up your heads, O gates" is siege language. That command is not gentle. Gates do not lift themselves unless authority confronts them. ownership is being reclaimed. access is being forced lawfully. Psalm 24 is not a worship chorus, it is a royal summons.

We see the resolution of a siege is not by human effort, but by Divine Force. This is when we rely on God, we must rely on Him and it is His good pleasure to keep us, feed us, protect us, and fight for us. He is a man of war; the Lord is His name. In your natural life if you had a certain expertise or forte but no one ever needed it, or asked you to use it, how would you feel? God wants to be God in our lives, and He has many attributes. Amen.

Psalm 23 prepares the table. Psalm 24 announces the King. Sustenance comes first — then sovereignty enters. The table steadies the people. The King of Glory ends the siege.

In faith if we rely on the One who is to be relied upon, even in **SEASONS OF SIEGE: GOD IS COMING.** You are allowed to sit and receive. You are allowed to be fed while God watches the field. He that watches Israel will never slumber nor sleep. The enemies are present, but God is hosting. When the enemy fully surrounds, diplomacy is over, strategy is exhausted, and alternatives are gone. So, Scripture never presents, *keep trying, find another way, do something clever, or wait and see indefinitely.* Instead, God does one of two things: He feeds you while they watch. He

23

empowers you to break through them. Anything else is human theorizing.

The enemy surrounds because they think you are about to starve, they think you are contained, they think you are desperate and they think they have won.

But Scripture flips it. Surrounding sets the table. Surrounding gathers the harvest. Surrounding removes ambiguity. The enemy never surrounds someone that God plans to abandon. They surround when they are trying to force surrender, they are trying to induce panic, they are trying to stop waiting on God and resting in Him.

In doing so, they expose themselves to one of the two outcomes above. When the enemy surrounds, God is no longer deciding whether or not to act. He is only planning HOW. If your alignment and your faith is right and your obedience is right toward God, He will come. Now how He resolves this siege is up to Him, not you or any other man. You have reached the place where your physical life must be touched by the Spirit of the Divine. Directly.

So, ask yourself these two questions: Am I being fed supernaturally? If yes, then sit. Don't move. Don't fight. Don't flee. The next question is: Am I being strengthened, sharpened, and authorized? If so, then: **2**. Rise. Arise & Thresh. Do not hesitate. A siege tests whether we remember where power has always belonged. God speaks once. Siege makes us listen twice. Power belongs to God.

THE FLOOR: ARISE AND THRESH

When under siege, surrounded by enemies, there is another possibility Scripture does not whisper; it announces it. Sometimes God allows the enemy to surround you not to starve you, not to test your endurance, not to see how long you can sit at the table, but because this is the moment He has been waiting for. The surrounding is not accidental. It is not miscalculation. It is not failure of protection. It is containment.

Unfortunately, there are some who run to the dark kingdom for whatever they are looking for, but mostly it is the dark kingdom that is running after us. When God made the Garden of Eden and put Adam and Eve in it, did they go looking for the serpent? No, the serpent came looking for them. So, they "gather" wherever mankind is.

We assume enemies surround because they are winning. Scripture shows the opposite. God often allows enemies to gather because He intends to deal with them at once. He is finished with delay. He wants no confusion about the outcome. He is removing escape routes from them. He is promoting you. How will you sit in dominion if no enemies are ever around for you to exert your authority over?

Scattered enemies require pursuit. Gathered enemies require authority.

Arise and thresh, O daughter of Zion: for I will make thine horn iron, and I will make thy hoofs brass: and thou shalt beat in pieces many people: and I will consecrate their gain unto the Lord, and their substance unto the Lord of the whole earth. (Micah 4:13)

That command is never given when danger is vague. It is given when the field is full. This is where you must not see your enemies as giants and yourself as a grasshopper. Yes, spiritual enemies have spiritual power. Yes, we are human and we don't oppose spiritual powers in the flesh, but in Christ, we are new creations and our weapons are now mighty through God to the pulling down of strongholds.

Threshing is not reaction, it is authorization. Threshing is not emotional. It is not revenge. It is not panic. Threshing only occurs when the enemy has shown their full hand, resistance is unmistakable, pressure has reached clarity, and God has decided the matter will not continue. Thank You, Lord! Threshing happens when the enemy is fully gathered, fear has burned off, timing is exact, and authorization has been clearly given.

God does not tell His people to thresh scattered enemies. He tells them to thresh when the harvest is ready. *"Arise and thresh..."* That command ends restraint. When God authorizes threshing: separation happens quickly, outcomes are irreversible, the matter does not need revisiting.

Threshing without authorization is disaster. And only restraint when threshing is commanded is disobedience.

I've not seen a third option--, just those two. When the enemy surrounds completely, Scripture does not offer clever alternatives. There is no strategizing your way out There is no negotiating relief or inventing solutions. There is no indefinite wait. It's now when God says it's now.

The moment has arrived.

Either God has seated you to be sustained or God has strengthened you to break through. The method He uses — angels, judgment, collapse, displacement — belongs to Him alone. Your responsibility is posture.

By threshing God is saying, *Enough*.

It is not warfare initiated by fear, it is action released by timing. God does not tell His people to thresh enemies who are still hiding. God never commands His people to hunt enemies. He *does* command His people to seek and save the lost. Judgment, pursuit, and hunting belong to God and His agents, not to redeemed humans.

Jesus states His mission plainly: *"For the Son of Man came to seek and to save the lost.* (Luke 19:10). And He transfers that mission to His followers thusly, *"Go therefore and make disciples of all nations..."* (Matthew 28:19). Notice what the commission includes. It says, go, preach, teach, heal, reconcile, rescue. It never includes hunt, pursue enemies, expose hidden adversaries, track opposition, or retaliate. The Church is sent outward toward people, not inward toward threats.

Scripture explicitly forbids humans from doing certain things. God is very clear about this boundary. Do not avenge yourselves... for it is written, Vengeance is Mine, I will repay,' says the Lord. (Romans 12:19)

Unless sent in wartime to capture a nation or its king, hunting enemies corrupts the human heart. It turns discernment into fixation. It replaces mission with suspicion. That is why God keeps that role for Himself. In Scripture, there are hunters. There are divine hunters, but they are not human. God Himself says,

God sends the hunters, warrior angels, divine carpenters. God defines the targets. God owns the action. Humans are never told to assume this role independently. John the Baptist was in the wilderness, but was he hunting? Not really, he was foraging for locusts and wild honey. The Israelites out of Egypt didn't even hunt, they had manna provided to them. And when they cried out for meat, God delivered that as well.

These hunters that God releases are angelic agents. Scripture repeatedly shows angels executing judgment, restraint, destruction, separation, enforcement. Some examples include, the angel who struck the Assyrian army (2 Kings 19), the angels in Egypt at Passover, and the angels in Revelation executing judgment.

Humans witness these acts. They do not initiate them. Humans should not hunt enemies because we lack omniscience. We may confuse people with *powers*. We may misinterpret timing. We may move into fear and act incorrectly. We may overreach authority. We may not be objective and may become emotional. We are not supposed to be judging other humans. And, as I always say, humans don't even know when enough punishment is enough; that's God's territory. We may not have any or enough or the right kind of Mercy and may overdo it.

This is why God marked Cain so no man would kill him, because most likely that's what a man would have done to him.

Instead, when opposition exists, believers are told to stand, resist, endure, flee temptation, guard the heart and preach anyway, keep doing good.

Resist the devil, and he will flee from you.(James 4:7)

So, we seek the lost. We can be fishers of men, but not hunters of men. God hunts for judgment. We obey our assignments. God handles enemies. We build tables and altars. God threshes on threshing floors and will scatter your enemies and sometimes that is exactly why they are drawn to you – and God knows it.

The Church rescues people. God removes opposition. That's divine division of labor. Scripture never commands God's people to hunt enemies. We are sent to seek the lost. Judgment and pursuit belong to God and His agents alone. When believers start hunting enemies, they abandon their mission and interfere with God's justice.

God has hunters. God has angels. God executes judgment. Redeemed humans are not deputized as hunters. They are ambassadors. And ambassadors do not hunt. They represent.

Threshing requires proximity, exposure, accountability and finality. Anointing is like the fragrance of the Lord. When you are anointed of God you naturally draw people unto you. Likewise, the enemy is drawn by that anointing as well. When enemies surround you, they believe you are contained, you are finished, you have no options. But Scripture shows something else is happening. God is locking the field. Nothing new enters. Nothing escapes. The issue will be resolved <u>here</u>.

450 Prophets of Baal gathered to defeat Elijah. Yes — that is one of the clearest siege-to-gathering-to-resolution moments in Scripture. Siege on Mount Carmel: When God Gathers the Opposition. Pay close attention here: this could be exactly what God is doing in your case. Elijah was not merely opposed, he was outnumbered, isolated, and publicly surrounded. There were 450 prophets of Baal and another 400 prophets of Asherah. Ahab, the hostile king. A compromised nation. A spiritual drought, and a powerful, visible altar war. If there was ever a moment that *looked* like defeat, this was it. Yet Scripture frames it differently.

Now therefore send and gather all Israel to me at Mount Carmel, and the four hundred and fifty prophets of Baal..." (1 Kings 18:19)

Who calls the gathering? Not Baal. Not Jezebel. Not the prophets. Elijah does — under God's authority. This is not Elijah walking into a trap. This is God locking the field.

God let them gather. God did not scatter Baal's prophets quietly; He did not deal with them privately. He did not reduce their numbers first. Oh no, He allowed maximum representation, full ritual, public spectacle, and complete exposure.

Why?

Because the question being answered was not about Baal. *Who is God?* **was the real question.** And the answer to that question required witnesses.

The siege was spiritual, not physical. Elijah wasn't starving, imprisoned, or .cornered geographically. But spiritually? The nation was besieged, truth was surrounded, allegiance was divided, rain was withheld.

Siege does not require chains — only constraint. Israel was constrained by deception. Elijah stood alone against a system. Prophets of God are called to do things like that; this is one of the reasons a **real** prophet of God may not run to a calling but from it. (Celebrity style prophets --- well, discern every *spirit.*)

Elijah did not hunt the prophets He did not track the prophets of Baal down. He did not expose them secretly, nor attack them in advance either with railing accusations, physically, or in any other way. He stood still until God gathered them.

God's people do not hunt enemies. God gathers them. Elijah didn't chase Baal. God brought Baal to Elijah, and the altar was the deciding place. Once gathered, Elijah did not debate. He repaired the altar. That's it. No argument. No persuasion. No theatrics.

The fire of the LORD fell... (1 Kings 18:38).

God answered **once.** Decisively. Publicly. After that, the people knew. The prophets were exposed. The drought broke. The siege ended. Mount Carmel shows us that gathering, no matter how large, does not mean or guarantee victory for the enemy. Numbers do not mean authority. Noise does not mean power. Spectacle does not equal truth. The Lord Our God is One; and He is Truth.

The prophets of Baal gathered because God was done waiting. When God answered, He did not need multiple attempts, prolonged warfare, or more force. One answer was enough. Baal's prophets gathered because God intended to answer publicly.

Elijah's moment was not reproducible by human effort. It was not a formula. It was not bravado. It was timing. When the siege reaches fullness, God gathers what He intends to answer and one answer is enough.

We dine. We sup, but we don't sit to long, recall the next chapter is about warfare and the King of Glory. Jumping ahead, threshing moments do not announce themselves quietly. If you feel strength replacing endurance, if restraint has burned off, if fear no longer governs your decisions, God may not be feeding you anymore. He may be arming you.

Threshing is decisive, it does not negotiate. Threshing does not explain itself. Threshing does not revisit outcomes. It is what it is. What is separated on a threshing floor is never recombined. This is why God waits so long before He authorizes it. Threshing ends cycles, breaks patterns, exposes what cannot remain, and closes doors permanently. This is not cruelty; it is Mercy with an ending.

Not everyone is called to *thresh*, but some are. Scripture does not make threshers out of everyone. But when God does, He prepares them in silence. He strengthens them in waiting. He removes their need for approval. He clarifies their authority. Threshers are not impulsive people; they are people who waited until the command came.

The most important discernment question is: Has God seated you to be sustained, or has He strengthened you to act? Both are holy. Both are necessary. But confusing them is dangerous. Sitting when God has said *Arise* delays justice. Threshing when God has said *Sit* creates destruction. This is why siege moments are sacred. They reveal posture.

The enemy surrounds because they believe containment equals control. They misread restraint as weakness. They mistake God's patience for absence. They do not know that this is the field God has chosen. And when God chooses the field, He also chooses how it will end.

Threshing requires proximity, force, and pressure. It requires the enemy to be gathered and also the thresher must have authorization.

Arise and thresh, daughter of Zion, for I will make your horn iron… (Micah 4:13A)

Threshing happens when fear is gone, else you will run from the enemy that should be running from you. Self-reliance is gone, you know you can't do this without God. Obedience is settled; God is in charge and you know it. It's time. God authorizes threshing, restraint ends. Sitting may no longer be your assignment. God may not be preparing a meal. Instead, He may be saying, **Arise. Thresh. Finish this**.

Let them be as chaff before the wind: and let the angel of the Lord chase them. (Psalm 35:5)

THE TABLE & THE THRESHING FLOOR

We return now to the table. But we do not return naïve. What once felt like rest now carries weight. What once felt like comfort now reveals purpose. Because a table, in Scripture, is never merely furniture. It is a prepared surface. And every prepared surface belongs to someone.

The table was always an altar. In the ancient world, a table was not first about eating. It was about presentation. Food was placed there. Offerings were placed there. Decisions were made there. Covenants were confirmed there. Altars and tables were often indistinguishable.

Both were raised, prepared, intentional, set apart, visible. Both existed for one reason and that was that something was about to be separated.

The threshing floor was also a table. A threshing floor was not hidden. It was flat, elevated, exposed to wind and intentionally prepared. Grain was brought there to be processed. What was useful remained. What was empty was removed. This was not destruction and it took discernment to decide what could be kept.

We read Psalm 23 as sheep-- hungry sheep. We hear the words, pasture, water, feeding, and rest. We think about ranchlands or farmlands, pastures, scenic fields and yesteryear, especially if we live in a city. God does feed His sheep. David a well-known shepherd was not only a shepherd, he was also a king. He understood tables as places of judgment and rule, not just nourishment. So when he says, *"You prepare a table before me in the presence of my enemies"* He is not describing escape. He is describing authority exercised openly. The enemies are not removed. They are made witnesses.

A table does not remove pressure — it redefines it. At a table you are seen, assessed, sustained and you are decided. The table does not ask whether enemies exist. It is blessed and by being blessed it declares that *This place belongs to God.* what belongs to God will not remain undefined.

There are seasons when the table exists to sustain. You sit. You receive. You do not act. You are kept alive while pressure remains. This is Mercy that prevents panic, premature action, bad agreements, and attempts at self-self-rescue. At this table, strength is preserved, and identity is protected. As well, fear is starved while the enemies watch. Nothing happens, yet.

The table becomes a threshing floor because tables do not remain static forever. The same surface that feeds also exposes. When God determines the time is full, the table shifts purpose. What was nourishment becomes separation. The wind rises. The weight falls. What cannot remain is removed. The table becomes a threshing floor without moving an inch. The difference is not the place. It is the command.

God uses the same place. God does not change locations unnecessarily. He prepares a place once — then changes what happens there. This is intentional because the enemy already recognizes the ground, the witnesses are already present, the authority is already established. God does not need to relocate to judge. He judges where He fed.

This is why the enemy surrounds the table. The enemy surrounds because they believe the table is delay, the feeding is indulgence and that waiting is weakness. They do not understand They are standing at an altar, and altars always require a response.

The question is no longer, *Is God here?* He is. But, the question is now, *Why has He prepared this surface?*

Answer these questions: Am I being sustained — or readied? Is strength being preserved — or sharpened? Is restraint still required — or has resolve replaced it? The table will tell you — if you listen.

By the Word of God, the table knows what happens next. Nothing placed on a threshing floor leaves unchanged. Nothing brought to God's table remains neutral. Both are places of truth, exposure, and outcome. The table is kind. The table is dangerous. Because once God prepares a surface, something will be decided there.

You were not brought to the table to be trapped. You were brought there to be fed, seen, separated, released — or restrained. The table and the threshing floor are not rivals. They are the same place at different moments. And the enemies who surround it will soon learn why.

SIGNS OF SIEGE

One of the clearest signs that a person is under siege is when asked what happened, they cannot explain it. Not because they are dishonest. They just don't know what happened, and that is not because they are in denial. But because there is no clean narrative to tell. If they start speaking spiritual jargon, people either won't understand them, or will look at them like they are crazy--, or both.

They did not fall blatantly into sin—they may not have sinned at all. They did not rebel. They did not make a catastrophic decision. They did not abandon Wisdom. If anything, they were more careful than usual. And yet something shifted. When people under siege try to describe their condition, they often say things such as, "I don't know how I got here." "Nothing actually happened." "There was no moment where things fell apart." "This shouldn't even be happening."

That confusion is not weakness. It is evidence. Sieges do not begin with events. They begin with containment. There is a collapse of familiar function. In most spiritual seasons, effort correlates with outcome.

When you pray, something changes. When you obey, doors open. When you move, momentum follows.

If there is a siege, that pattern is suddenly and sometimes quietly broken. The tools that once worked still function in theory, but no longer produce movement. Prayer still reaches God, but does not change conditions. Wisdom still matters but does not accelerate timing. Faith still exists but does not translate into progress.

This is deeply unsettling, especially for people who have learned to steward their lives well. It feels illogical. Unfair. Out of sequence. This shouldn't be happening. This can't be happening. *Pinch me?*

It produces a dangerous question: *What if I'm losing something I used to have?* But siege is not loss of capacity. It is suspension of function.

A person could fall under siege by being called the wrong name in a sustained way. A person could fall under siege by being misnamed. A person could fall under siege by being abused, misused, brainwashed or misidentified. Those types of sieges are not from God; they are from evil agents and sponsored by the dark kingdom.

When or if a siege is from God, He may be allowing interruption because it is is one of God's least explained mercies. When God interrupts what once worked, it is not because the tool is broken. It is because the outcome can no longer be achieved through that tool alone. What once required Faith, obedience, and or discipline may now require Divine Intervention. God may be establishing a new timing. There may be exposure of something beyond your control.

Or, God makes things stop that you need to stop doing, or doing in the way you are doing them.

If familiar methods continued to work, you would eventually attribute relief to effort—even if you thanked God afterward. A siege removes that possibility. It creates a condition where only God's movement can end it, and therefore God's involvement cannot be minimized, shared, or internalized as personal achievement.

There is an illusion of regression. When what used to work stops working, many people assume regression. They think, "I've lost ground." "I'm back where I started." "Something has drained out of me." "Where are my virtues?" Where is my star?" " Where is my Glory that God gave me?" Or this one, "I used to walk in favor."

But regression has markers. There is moral decay. There is disobedience. There is neglect. In a siege, none of those are present. You are not going backward. You are being held in place. This distinction matters, because trying to "recover" something you have not lost wastes strength you need to endure.

Explanation fails in a siege. Human understanding depends on sequence. We expect cause and effect. We expect action to lead to results. We expect mistakes to lead to consequences, well for others anyway. Sieges violate sequence. I pressed the remote—why isn't the TV coming on? Sieges insert pressure without an initiating error. They remove effect from effort. They sever explanation from experience. That is why people under siege struggle to tell their story. The language of cause and effect no longer applies. Said plainly – it just doesn't make sense! And that creates internal distress.

The mind wants coherence. The spirit wants assurance. The body wants relief. A siege offers none of these immediately. Instead, it demands trust without comprehension.

There is danger in forcing meaning too early. When explanation fails, people often rush to interpretation. They assign meaning prematurely thinking things like, "God must be displeased." "I must have missed something." "This must be punishment."

These interpretations feel grounding, but they are false anchors. In Scripture, meaning is often revealed after relief—not during containment. Trying to understand a siege while inside it often leads to distortion, not clarity. This is why God does not require understanding in this season. He requires stability.

What you are experiencing is structural, not personal. A siege is a structural condition imposed from outside—not a reflection of internal failure. Think of a city under siege: The walls still stand. The people still exist. The leadership remains. The identity of the city does not change. What changes is movement. Supply is restricted. The exits are blocked. Time is distorted; it stretches. Nothing is wrong with the city. It is simply enclosed.

I am not losing what God gave me. The next movement requires His hand alone.

WHAT USED TO WORK NO LONGER WORKS

The forms a siege can take are not defined by *what* is affected, but by how pressure is applied. Still, sieges often concentrate in one or more areas of life. Knowing where the pressure is focused helps you respond wisely—without mislabeling yourself. Most people experience more than one type at the same time.

A physical siege is when the body becomes the enclosure. Chronic fatigue. Illness with no clear resolution. Decreased capacity. Physical limits that restrict movement. This siege tempts people to override the body or spiritualize depletion. Key danger: ignoring limits to escape pressure. This is why some older or sick people decide to FORCE themselves to do what the doctor said don't do, or what they can't do. They do not like the siege and who can blame them. But we can understand and pray accordingly.

Financial Siege - Resources are restricted. Money doesn't stretch. Money doesn't work anymore, or worse, you don't have any, or you don't have enough. Income feels capped. What income? You used to have an income, but where did it go?

Unexpected expenses, over and again. You feel that this is spiritual because in the natural it's quiet, nothing is happening. Everything looks normal on the surface. You're not shopping, you're not buying anything more than you used to, you might even be buying less, but where is your money?

Help exists, but at a cost. This siege tempts people toward high-risk "solutions" (gambling, bad contracts, desperate agreements). Warning: Do not trade *long-term stability for short-term relief.*

Social / Relational Siege - Movement is restricted through people. Gatekeepers. Authority figures. Family systems. Institutions. Abusive spouses or significant others. Manipulative helpers. This siege tempts people to comply to escape, even when compliance costs dignity or authority.

Warning: Do not accept *rescue that replaces autonomy.* Gatekeepers and that one soul. Sometimes a siege is not designed to stop a crowd, sometimes it is designed to stop one connection. This is one of the least understood forms of gatekeeping, especially within families. Family gatekeepers rarely look hostile. They look concerned, protective, cautious, or "just trying to keep the peace." But their effect can be the same as a locked gate. They control access.

Gatekeeping shows up in families because families have existing hierarchies, unspoken rules, and assigned roles. When one person carries clarity, discernment, or spiritual authority that does not fit the system, pressure forms around them — often quietly. The goal is not always to silence them entirely. Often the goal is simpler, such as limit who can reach them or limit who they can reach. Keep influence contained and keep insight from transferring. This is how a family can tolerate someone's presence but resist their impact.

The one other spiritual person in the family matters deeply. In many families, there is only one other person capable of recognizing what you carry. They often are not the loudest or most 'religious', but the one with eyes to see. They could be the one to speak into your life or you into theirs. The family may try to keep you from Grandma because they want inheritance of things and stuff from Grandma while the spiritual person in the family is not even thinking like that. The other spiritual person in the family just wants to spend time with Grandma, but that's not how those who want financial inheritance see it. Grandma could carry legacy or a mantle, that needs to be transferred to the one they are trying to keep her from.

That person becomes significant not because of numbers, but because of spiritual *recognition*. And recognition threatens gatekeeping.

Gatekeepers fear transfer, and that they will miss out. Gatekeepers are rarely afraid of discussion. They are afraid of the transfer of clarity, courage, discernment, authority, spiritual language, and identity permission.

A single authentic connection can undo years of quiet containment. Ways of gatekeeping include, visits getting stopped or interrupted/ shortened or monitored. Conversations get monitored. misunderstandings get stirred.

distance is encouraged "for everyone's good." Narratives are shaped before contact occurs. The aim is not confrontation. It is prevention.

This is a siege pattern. This form of siege restricts access rather than movement, isolates selectively, pressures relationally rather than physically, operates quietly over time. Often it goes unnamed because it looks *normal*. But when someone finally recognizes it, the pattern becomes visible. And once visible, it loses power. Exposure to light always destroys the works of darkness.

Some connections are delayed not because God is withholding, but because a person may not be ready. It's too soon for recognition; it would be rejected. Protection is needed first, or the cost would be too high, prematurely. When the time is right, the gatekeeping is exposed without confrontation.

Gatekeepers are not always malicious; many times, they are clueless and don't even know they are being used by the enemy. Often, they are afraid, invested, or protecting a system that feels necessary to them. You can pray against closed gates and evil gatekeepers—not against flesh and blood, although a gatekeeper is empowered by a strongman and the gatekeeper is a human being. Whether they know they are gatekeeping or not, pray. If God is willing to allow years of pressure around one connection, then, one soul matters. Each soul matters. And when that soul finally says, *"Now I see,"* the siege has already done its work.

Gatekeeping delays connection, but it cannot prevent recognition forever. *Sometimes the siege is not about stopping the message — it is about delaying the moment one person finally recognizes it.*

Emotional Siege - Internal pressure intensifies in the emotional siege. Emotional numbness or overload has started. There is grief without release. Anxiety without clear cause. Suppressed emotion due to feeling like you're in survival mode. This siege tempts people to self-medicate or shut down discernment and start acting in the flesh or through their emotions. Girl, I just got me a glass of wine and then another one. This is a mistake; you have to stay clear-eyed and clear thinking. Resist the temptation to make *decisions made to stop feeling.*

Mental Siege - The mind becomes crowded in the mental siege. There is overthinking, rumination, anxiety, worry, fretting, and the inability to decide. There is mental exhaustion, loss of clarity. This siege tempts people to **force** meaning, assign blame, or rush conclusions. Key danger: *confusing mental noise with insight.*

Spiritual Siege - Access feels restricted. Prayer feels dry. Scripture feels flat. God feels silent. Former spiritual practices lose traction. This siege tempts people to perform spiritually or assume abandonment. Key danger: *turning relationship into transaction.*

The most important clarification is that the presence of a siege does not mean something is wrong in that area. It means pressure has been *applied* there. A financial siege does not mean poor stewardship. A spiritual siege does not mean weak faith. A relational siege does not mean bad character. It means that area has become the point of control, containment if an enemy is causing the siege.

If it is God, then it may be for the purpose of refinement or restructuring.

ANSWERS UNDER SIEGE

In Daniel 10, Daniel fasts and prays for understanding. He is not rebuked. He is not corrected. He is not being punished. In fact, the angel explicitly tells him:

From the first day that you set your heart to understand and humbled yourself before your God, your words were heard, and I have come because of your words. (Daniel 10:12)

God heard immediately. The response was released immediately. The delay was not on Daniel's end. So, that rules out unbelief, sin, or incorrect prayer.

The angel continues:

But the prince of the kingdom of Persia withstood me twenty-one days... (Daniel. 10:13)

This tells us something extremely important: The resistance was not against Daniel's devotion, it was against the *delivery* of the answer. That is classic siege logic — pressure applied to the *route*, not the source. As a matter of fact, the enemy may not be able to oppose your person—you are redeemed from the Curse of the Law. Amen. But others around you, destiny helpers, systems, situation, those who should be writing your check, or releasing your money – if they are not saved and in Christ, they could be used by the enemy to affect your life and your outcomes. Pray for them, for their sake, yes, but also as it affects you, your purpose, life, ministry, and destiny.

Daniel still had uninterrupted access to God. The answer was released so Daniel had his authorization, he just didn't know it yet because the transmission was resisted. It looked like God was the problem; Ultimately if the enemy can get you to doubt God, the battle against you is won.

Finally, breakthrough came through external intervention (Archangel Michael) resolved it.

Daniel did not "push harder" to break the siege. He remained steady; he continued to fast and pray. He didn't go all frantic and escalate into some new form of fasting or praying or other weird, invented discipline. He didn't accuse God—which would have been very stupid. (I told God. (Oh, sit down.)). Daniel didn't try some work-around to self-rescue. He didn't make any threats or panic declarations. He didn't revile dignities, calling those in the kingdom of darkness derogatory names. He stayed governed.

Who in the Bible ever "cussed the devil out"? We do not revile dignities. Any entity that exists is because God allows it. Talk to God; remain respectful.

The Prince of Persia was besieging the answer. The answer was contained. Progress was restricted. Resistance was strategic. Timing was affected. The blockage was external. Daniel was in Prince of Persia territory—he was in captivity, so that is a whole other level of siege when your siege is under siege.

Some forms of captivity are inherited, not chosen. Others are entered without discernment. Wisdom asks God where to live, not just how to survive once there. Not every siege is about you — but every territory must be interpreted.

The Bible doesn't say that Daniel was under demonic attack or that God was testing Daniel's endurance, or that fasting moved God's hand, although I've heard it preached that way—especially in January. This siege was a result of cosmic resistance to transmission, not spiritual punishment. Many people misuse Daniel 10 to justify striving harder under siege, which is opposite of what the passage teaches.

Daniel was not unheard, delayed, or corrected. His answer was resisted in transit. This reveals that some sieges do not block access to God — they obstruct the delivery of what God has already released. And this kind of delay is not resolved by panic or force, but by remaining aligned while God resolves what lies outside human reach.

Daniel did not know about the Prince of Persia until after the answer arrived. We can then surmise that you do not need full spiritual explanations to remain faithful under delay. Daniel stayed steady without insight. That is faith. Without faith it is impossible to please God.

The explanation of what had happened was came later. That, too, is siege Wisdom. In this case, the siege was on the answer, not on the man, not on his faith, and it wasn't placed by God directly. Daniel had ended up in Babylon because of the idolatry of that nation and God had warned them over and again. Daniel in Babylon was collateral damage.

Spiritual siege means something spiritual is causing the siege. This is not about a person being tied up or locked away somewhere. In the natural, all things could look normal, but there is a spiritual component to the problem, obstacle, delay, or stagnation. Spiritual siege is not visible confinement, punishment, or personal failure. It is not physical restraints. It is invisible containment caused by an opposing spiritual agency, operating at the level of *delay, obstruction, resistance, or interference* — while natural life may appear normal.

A spiritual siege does not require a person to be physically trapped, isolated, or visibly attacked. In fact, many spiritual sieges occur while life appears outwardly functional and uninterrupted. A spiritual siege exists when access to God remains open, obedience remains intact, character is not under correction, and circumstances basically look ordinary. While at the same time, progress, movement, or delivery is being resisted by an unseen opposing force.

The siege is not against the person's existence — it is against what is moving through them or toward them. Nothing *looks* "wrong" in the natural, therefore people assume the delay is psychological. Some may think it is laziness or some other mental or emotional problem. It could be that the person is under siege. For example, I've noticed people from other countries, who have everything they need to do things that would impact their life favorably, but they never do them. Instead of being judgmental, which I was at first, I've had to look closer and ask the Lord, "Are they under judgment from You? Are they under siege? Do they need individual deliverance, or is it a territorial, national, ancestral, generational, family, captivity, or siege problem? Why do they look or act 'stuck' but they don't seem stuck in the natural? Once we get the answer from God, then we are informed as to how to pray, if that person wants you to pray for or with them.

Others assume that stuckness is God's timing. Can't blame it all on God because without discernment how will we know the source of the delay? Without even trying, a person even under siege could look the same or they could look natural or normal – at least for a while. The person under siege may blame themselves. Helpers may offer advice that doesn't apply. Spiritual siege is so disorienting. Nothing is broken — yet nothing is moving.

A delay does not always mean God is silent. Sometimes it means delivery is being resisted. Daniel's life was not shut down. His access to God was not blocked. His obedience was not questioned. Yet something external was actively withholding movement. That is spiritual siege.

Misnaming this kind of siege leads people to repent for sins they didn't commit, strive harder when stillness is required, accuse God unfairly, accept bad "solutions" out of frustration, abandon assignments prematurely, or repeat cycles. Correct naming restores authority without panic.

A spiritual siege occurs when an unseen opposing force resists movement, delivery, or outcome, even though access to God, obedience, and outward life remain intact. No, you are not cray cray. You are not tripping. You are not failing; there really may be a siege that has you corralled.

51

THE INTERNAL SIEGE

However, not every delay is a *spiritual* siege. Not every obstacle has an external agent. This is where prayer and discernment must come in. Wisdom is not in obsession with the unseen, but it is with accurate naming. Unless you name a thing, you cannot manage it. Adam was allowed to name everything, and what he named it, that was its name.

Daniel was in captivity by no fault of his own; he was in collective captivity with the rest of Judah. So he was under siege, within a siege. Getting out of siege while in captivity is another whole thing. Daniel was under siege *within* a larger, collective siege, one he did not cause, could not exit, and was not assigned to personally resolve.

Siege *within* siege: Daniel was taken into captivity by no fault of his own. He was swept up in collective judgment on Judah, living inside a system he did not create. He was faithful inside an unfaithful nation and obedient inside a disobedient generation. Daniel was under siege inside a siege.

The Babylonian/Persian captivity was the *macro-siege*. The resistance to his answered prayer was a *micro-siege*. They operated simultaneously.

this is a different category entirely. Daniel's situation proves something critical: Not all sieges are meant to be escaped. Some are meant to be endured faithfully while God works above, around, and beyond them.

Joseph was successful and operated well in prison and in Egypt once he started using his spiritual gifts.

Daniel was never promised immediate release from captivity, personal exemption from national consequence, nor relocation to friendly territory. Yet God promised him was promised favor, access, revelation, authority, and preservation. He ultimately was promoted to satrap of a Babylonian territory.

Getting out of siege while remaining in captivity; that's really a *thing*. Daniel did not get *out* of captivity. He got free *within* it. He experienced clarity while constrained, authority while restrained, limited favor while restricted, revelation while delayed, Peace while surrounded. So, when we talk about "ending siege," Daniel teaches us that sometimes the siege that ends is not the one you are living in, but the one operating *within* it.

The answer arrived. Understanding came. Authority was restored. But captivity remained. Daniel was okay.

This corrects a dangerous assumption that many people have. *If God answers me, my environment must change.*

Daniel disproves that. God answered Daniel without changing his zip code. This tells us that breakthrough can be geographic but it is not always. Freedom is not always circumstantial. Deliverance is not always extraction, but it would be nice. Authority is not always relocation. Sometimes God resolves what is movable and leaves what is not for later.

That is not failure; that is Wisdom.

Daniel was faithful inside a siege he did not cause and could not escape. His obedience did not remove the captivity, but it preserved clarity, authority, and peace within it. Some sieges end by lifting. Others end by losing their power over you.

Daniel teaches us that God does not require escape to prove faithfulness. Daniel was still God's agent within a macro siege. Is this not symbolic of Nebuchadnezzar's fire, but the men in the fire were unbound and walking around in the flames? We are also God's agents: we are in the world, but not *of* it. Sometimes the most profound victory is staying aligned, clear, obedient and sane, while history marches on to the fullness of Time.

God does not always remove the outer captivity in order to resolve the inner one. Some are sent or born into enemy territory and remain there as agents of change, or activity, of evangelism, intercession, or deliverance. So are watchmen. Sometimes the outer siege is caused by an inner one-- faulty thinking. for example, thinking that God is not able--- but He is, but if we don't ask, or avail ourselves in faith, the outer situation will manifest.

Sometimes the outer captivity remains while the inner one is resolved. Sometimes the outer siege exists *because* the inner one has not been settled.

Both are true. Scripture shows both patterns. When the outer siege is *not* caused by the inner one. Daniel's captivity was collective, not personal. Paul and Silas were unjustly imprisoned; the outer situation did not reflect faulty faith. In these cases, God resolved the inner condition (clarity, authority, peace) without immediately changing the outer environment.

When the outer siege *is* caused by an inner one, this is the other side. There are times when faulty thinking, unbelief about God's nature, passivity disguised as humility, assumptions about limitation, and unasked-for help ...create conditions where the outer situation is allowed to persist.

It's not because God is unable, but it is because access is unused. Scripture is very plain about this.

You do not have because you do not ask. (James 4:2)

God's ability was never in question. The issue was engagement. The subtle inner siege: misjudging God's willingness or ability. One of the most common *inner* sieges is not rebellion, it's low expectation. Thoughts like *"God probably won't..." "This is just how it is." "I don't want to bother God." "I should handle this myself."* Those thoughts feel reasonable. They feel mature and responsible. But they quietly restrict access. And over time, the outer situation hardens into something that looks immovable.

Israel's repeated lesson is shown clearly in their wilderness after Egypt. God was able. God was present. God was willing. But unbelief limited what they entered. They could not enter in because of doubt, unbelief, and either not knowing how to lean on God or instead only leaning to their own understanding. (Hebrews 3:19)

55

Notice God's power was not diminished. The promise was not revoked. The limitation was internal. That's inner siege manifesting outwardly.

"Every bad situation is your fault," or "Think right and everything changes." Discern whether the siege is external, internal, or layered — and respond accordingly.

God does not always remove the outer captivity in order to resolve the inner one. But at times, the outer siege persists because an inner one remains — often rooted in faulty thinking about who God is and what He is willing to do. Faith does not create God's ability. It avails itself of it.

Is this something God is sustaining me through? Or is this something God is waiting for me to bring to Him in faith

I asked a girl on New Years Day if she had champagne to toast in the New Year, she said, Champagne is for rich people, (not for her.)

Identity can function as an inner siege. When she said, *"Champagne is for rich people."* She was making an identity declaration, not a financial statement. *"That world is not mine." "That belongs to people like them, not people like me." "I am not included in that category."* No one excluded her in that moment. She excluded herself — preemptively. That is inner siege at work.

Identity-based sieges are so powerful because identity beliefs don't feel like chains. They feel like common sense. They feel like obedience—I'm doing what Grandma said or what my parents told me. They sound like realism,

56

humility practicality, "knowing your place," and being responsible. They are dangerous because they are insidious and do not look like weapons formed against you, but they may keep a person under siege.

They don't argue with God outright. They simply never ask. And what is not asked for is not received except in cases of Divine Grace and Mercy. Many times, God is simply waiting for us to ask. Many times asking is a marker of Wisdom, knowledge and identity. We know who we are in God. We know the Word; we know what we can have, and we are timely: we know that it is time or okay to ask God for what we need or want.

Identity siege manifests outwardly over time, with beliefs like that which restrict what a person reaches for, limit what feels "appropriate," shrink imagination, and can really shrink a person. They reduce expectation, and normalize lack. Eventually, the outer world conforms to the inner assumption, not because God agreed, but because access was never availed. This connects directly to Scripture when the Israelites in the wilderness didn't say, "God cannot." They said, "We are grasshoppers." (Numbers 13:33) That's identity speech that shaped outcome.

Their inner identity produced an outer delay.

People under identity siege are often faithful, moral, hardworking, and sincere. They just don't believe certain doors are *for them*. They say when you get to Heaven and see all that God has prepared for you that you never got because you never asked for it, you'll be shocked. They didn't think good was for them, so they don't knock. That's conditioning producing real-life limitations.

Sometimes the outer siege is sustained by an inner one — not because God is unwilling, but because identity has quietly decided what is "not for me." Faith is not pretending to be someone else. It is agreeing with who God already says you are. Recognition is the first crack in an inner siege. Identity-based sieges don't shout. They whisper rules. And the moment those rules are questioned — not mocked, not judged, their opposing authority weakens.

Knowing God is the first step in knowing yourself.

...but the people that do know their God shall be strong, and do exploits. (Daniel11:32B)

RELATIONSHIPS UNDER SIEGE

Relationships are one of the *primary theaters* where siege shows up, and people misinterpret it constantly. Not every relationship that struggles is under spiritual siege. Not every siege means the relationship should continue. Discernment matters here, because relationships amplify consequences more than almost anything else.

1. Three Possible Sources of Relationship Siege

A. God Is Saying **"No"**. Sometimes the siege is not opposition, it is prevention. Indicators are the following: clarity never stabilizes, Peace does not settle, but if it comes, it must be from you. Alignment requires self-betrayal, the relationship pulls you away from obedience. The "yes" always has to be manufactured. God's "no" is not cruelty. Many times, it is protection from a future you cannot yet see. Trust in the LORD with all your heart… He will make your paths straight. (Proverbs 3:5–6)

When God is saying no, pressing harder does not produce fruit, or a diamond, it produces damage.

The relationship is under external opposition. Indicators are both parties are aligned and growing, but Peace exists underneath the pressure. Opposition is external, not

59

relational. Clarity increases with prayer, not confusion. Neither person has to abandon integrity. This kind of siege targets what the relationship would become, not the people themselves. God loves when two become one, and the devil hates it, so don't think that after you get married there won't be any more spiritual opposition. But even here, stillness and timing matter more than force.

Anti-Marriage or Anti-Covenant Patterns can exist or be at work in a family. If you see repeated relational outcomes this may be why. Signs include near-misses, attraction to unavailable partners, relationships that collapse at the same stage, fear of permanence, and internal resistance when things become stable. This is not bad luck. It is often unexamined inheritance. Pray foundational prayers for your family as well as your spouse's. Pray together, as **one**.

Relationship siege often feels like emotional exhaustion, constant misunderstanding, timing that never aligns, pressure to compromise values, urgency to "make it work." fear of losing the opportunity.

Do not rush into commitment to end anxiety if a relationship is under siege. Notice red flags; read the signs along the way. Do not blame yourself for God's restraint. Do not override Peace to preserve attachment. Marriage is not deliverance and all this opposition will not magically disappear after, I do's. It may get worse. Marriage does not heal siege unless you are sent by God. If you are a kinsman redeemer, then marriage is the solution. If you are Hosea marrying Gomer, then problems solved by virtue of doing what God said to do, else, there is work to do. Else, marriage merely magnifies whatever already exists.

Discernment questions that protect you. Does this relationship bring clarity or confusion? Does obedience to God become easier or harder with this person? Do I feel more myself — or less? Am I being asked to shrink, rush, or prove? Does stillness strengthen the relationship — or weaken it? God does not require chaos to bring covenant.

Letting go ends the siege. Sometimes the siege lifts not because the relationship succeeds, but because it ends. That does not mean failure, but then again, it could mean failure. When God removes a relationship, He is not subtracting love — He is **removing interference and alignment is restored**. Make sure it is God that is removing the relationship.

There are other bad actors in the world who may want to break you and your spouse apart. Be wise. (see my other books on relationships in the credits such as *spirit spouse* books, **Astral Projected Spirit Spouse Must Die, The Spirit of Anti-Marriage, Prayers for Marriage in the Courts of Heaven, The Battlefield of Marriage, Unauthorized Use, Six Men Short, By Means of a Whorish Father, The Dangers of Sex.** etc.)

Sometimes we have to wait on God. Sometimes we have to look deeper to make sure there is no other interference. He who believes will not act hastily. (Isaiah 28:16)

A relationship under siege must be discerned, not rescued. God does not ask us to bind ourselves to confusion in order to prove faith. Love that requires you to abandon peace is not from God.

Prayer for Singles Relationship

God of Wisdom and faithfulness, I come to You without fear of being forgotten and without rushing to secure what You have not yet given.

You know my desire for companionship, for covenant, for shared life — and You also know the cost of choosing wrongly.

If a relationship is being restrained because it is not from You, give me the strength to release it without bitterness, comparison, or self-blame.

If I am waiting because You are protecting me — from patterns I cannot yet see or futures I am not meant to carry — teach me to trust Your restraint as care, not denial.

If forces from my past, my family, or my history have shaped what I believe is "for people like me," gently correct those lies. Restore my sense of worth, belonging, and expectancy.

Guard me from settling out of loneliness or rushing out of fear. Guard me from making permanent decisions to escape temporary pressure.

If waiting is my season, let it be peaceful, not punishing. Let it strengthen discernment, not diminish hope. I trust You to bring the right connection at the right time without my striving, forcing, or proving.

I place my future in Your hands and refuse to believe that delay means absence. In the Name of Jesus, **Amen.**

Prayer for Marrieds When a Relationship Is Under Siege

God of covenant and truth, I come to You acknowledging that marriage, too, can experience pressure, resistance, and strain. You see what is happening beneath the surface — the misunderstandings, the fatigue, the patterns that repeat, and the weight that feels heavier than it should.

If this pressure is meant to refine us, teach us how to grow without hardening and to listen without defending.

If opposition is external — from stress, history, interference, or spiritual resistance — give us discernment to stand together without turning against one another.

Expose any patterns we have inherited that undermine unity, trust, or safety. Heal what we cannot heal on our own.

Remove the urge to escape, to blame, or to withdraw emotionally in self-protection. Restore peace to our communication. Restore clarity to our decisions. Restore tenderness where distance has formed.

If restraint is required, teach us patience. If correction is needed, grant humility. If intervention is necessary, bring it without delay. We place our marriage under Your covering as a covenant You are faithful to sustain.

Guard what You joined together. Strengthen us without breaking us. And let no siege have the final word over what You have established. In the Name of Jesus, **Amen.**

THE IMPOSSIBILITY OF SELF-RESCUE

A siege creates a very specific kind of pressure. It is not the pressure to sin. It is not the pressure to rebel. It is not even the pressure to give up faith. It is the pressure to rescue yourself. Self-rescue in a siege rarely looks sinful. It looks *practical*. It sounds like Wisdom. It often feels overdue. This is what makes it so dangerous.

We have not the power to redeem ourselves. No clearer example than when Jesus had to come redeem mankind back to the Father.

Self-rescue is because of self-reliance and that can lead to pride and even idolatry if you think you are *all that*. Remember in the wilderness the Israelites refused to lean on or rest in God. As time passes without movement, the mind begins to search for exits—not because they are right, but because they are *available*. The pressure says, "You can't stay here forever." "Something has to change." "God helps those who help themselves." "At least this would give you relief." Under siege conditions, relief starts to look like salvation. But relief is not deliverance. And movement is not progress. A siege does not always tempt you with rebellion-

-,   although   it   can.
But it can also tempt you with premature solutions.

Self-rescue is rarely dramatic abandonment of faith. More often, it takes subtler forms before clarity returns. accepting lesser outcomes to end pressure, explaining away restraint as I'm just keeping it real. Reducing expectations for peace. Compromising posture for momentum. Choosing movement over remaining aligned with God – which is rebellion. Although these may not feel sinful; they feel *necessary*. And that is the trap.

Self-rescue fails in a siege. In Scripture, sieges end one of two ways: By intervention, or by collapse. Self-rescue always leads to collapse—if not immediately, then eventually. *Why?* Because a siege is not something you escape from. It is something lifted.

You cannot dig your way out of a condition designed to be removed from above. You cannot negotiate your way out of containment imposed from outside. You cannot out-strategize a season governed by timing rather than effort. Self-rescue assumes the problem is solvable by action. A siege proves otherwise.

Self-rescue does not just end the siege. It ends formation. What is being protected in a siege is not merely an outcome—it is authority, alignment, and testimony. When a person self-rescues the pressure lifts. The lesson remains incomplete. The authority does not transfer. The cycle eventually repeats. This is why some people experience repeated enclosures in different forms.

They escaped the pressure—but not the purpose.

God allows the pressure to intensify. The pressure increases because the temptation to self-rescue increases. God does not increase pressure to punish. He allows it to reveal. At a certain point, the question is no longer *"Can you endure?"* It becomes, *"Will you trust Me more than your own relief?"*

This is where many faithful people falter—not because they stop believing, but because they start *managing*. They exchange surrender for control. They exchange trust for contingency plans. They exchange obedience for outcomes. And they call it Wisdom.

The impossibility is the point. A siege is designed to feel impossible. Not discouraging—impossible. When all reasonable options fail, when every responsible path closes, when even your best thinking produces no movement, the message is clear: This will not end by your hand.

That realization is not despair. It is alignment. The impossibility removes pride without humiliating you. It removes control without condemning you. It positions you for relief without demanding performance.

Remaining in a siege does not mean doing nothing. It means refusing to abandon posture. Remaining looks like not forcing answers, not trying to force God. Not begging and whining. It looks like knowing who you are in Christ; not shrinking identity. It looks like standing and standing therefore. It looks like not lowering obedience to buy relief, not leaving alignment just to feel movement, and not calling compromise *peace.*

Remaining is not passive; it is faith under conditions of restraint.

Hold these Truths: If self-rescue were possible, the siege would not exist. If effort could end it, it would already be over. If strategy were enough, God would not have allowed enclosure. The fact that rescue feels impossible is not a failure of faith. It is the confirmation that relief must come from God alone. Be still and know that I am God.

Pray this: I will not rescue myself. I will not trade alignment for relief. I trust that what God will lift, I do not need to escape. In the Name of Jesus, Amen.

There comes a moment in every true siege when effort finally fails. This is not laziness, disobedience, or ignorance. This is not giving up, it is giving in to God. When you reach the honest realization: this cannot be fixed from inside the system and put your faith on the Lord, then you have already won the siege.

In *Nehemiah 5*, the people reach that moment when they are rebuilding the wall. There is outward progress and the morale should be high, but beneath the surface, a quieter catastrophe is unfolding. Their lands are mortgaged. Their children are being taken as collateral. Their inheritance is being consumed to survive the present. They cry out — not because they are unwilling to work, but because they have worked and still cannot recover what has been lost. The essence of their cry is devastatingly simple:

We do not have the power to redeem ourselves. This is the moment that defines a true siege.

Siege is not hardship; it is the collapse of self-redemption. Many difficulties can be solved with Wisdom, effort, or repentance. A siege cannot. A siege is revealed when obedience does not undo the debt, effort does not restore inheritance, righteousness does not reverse captivity, perseverance does not produce freedom. It's when you may be asking God, "Hey, what's going on here? I've done everything I know how to do. Why isn't anything working anymore?"

The people in Nehemiah were not rebellious, nor extravagant. They were not faithless, nor foolish. They were not refusing responsibility; they were diligent. Yet, they were mortgaged. And a mortgage cannot be undone by willpower. That is what makes a siege different from struggle. The deeper problem was this: Even with protection restored, the people themselves were still bound. Security without redemption is not freedom. Structure without release is not restoration. And that is the truth humanity has lived with ever since Eden.

What Israel experienced economically and socially in Nehemiah, humanity experiences spiritually. And they could not escape on their own. Inheritance was mortgaged. Freedom was lost through no single personal act. Captivity was embedded in systems larger than the individual. Debt we, ourselves did not originate — yet cannot pay. This is why Scripture does not present salvation as self-improvement; it is presented as Redemption.

Redemption assumes that something was lost. Something is owned by another. Something cannot be reclaimed by effort. A price must be paid externally. This is the siege mankind was locked into--, inability to rescue ourselves.

It is why Jesus had to come. Jesus did not come because humanity needed better teaching, though He was a Master Teacher. Teaching assumes capacity. He came because humanity was mortgaged — like the families in Nehemiah. He did not come to show us how to climb out. He came to buy us back. That is why Scripture calls Him, Redeemer, Ransom, Advocate, Deliverer.

A Redeemer only exists where self-rescue is impossible. If humanity could save itself, the Cross would be unnecessary.

LORD, BUY ME BACK FROM WHEREVER THEY HAVE SOLD ME, IN THE NAME OF JESUS. AMEN.

When people are under siege today — spiritually, financially, relationally — the greatest temptation is not despair, it is the temptation of self-salvation. The lies sound like: "I just need to try harder." "I must not be praying correctly." "If I fix myself, this will lift." "I should be able to solve this."

But Nehemiah exposes the truth, there are situations where trying harder deepens the damage. Because effort applied to an unredeemable system only tightens the bind.

That is why bad offers appear. That is why shortcuts tempt. That is why desperation whispers, *Do something.* And that is why Scripture repeatedly says:

Be still.

69

Stillness is not passivity; it is the refusal to pretend you can redeem yourself. Stillness, standing and standing therefore is warfare. Warfare leaning on the Lord. Continued attempts at self-rescue smacks of pride, and God resists the prideful, but He will run to a man of humble heart. He will rescue the humble.

> Humble yourselves therefore under the mighty hand of God, that he may exalt you in due time (1 Peter 5:6)

Siege is not always meant to be escaped immediately. Sometimes it exists to reveal the truth we resist: I need a Redeemer, not a strategy. Or, better: I HAVE A REDEEMER; shall I not see Him as Redeemer? Siege is when you must work out your salvation with fear and trembling. For real.

This is not humiliation. It is alignment with reality. The people in Nehemiah did not solve the mortgage problem by effort. It required intervention. Correction. Advocacy. Authority beyond the individual. That is the same pattern God uses in salvation.

If you are under siege and nothing you do seems to move it, ask this question carefully:

Is this something God is asking me to manage, or something He is revealing I cannot redeem myself from? Those are very different situations. One calls for Wisdom. The other calls for trust in redemption. Trying to apply effort where redemption is required leads to exhaustion. Receiving redemption where it is offered leads to peace.

The truth at the center of this book is that a siege is not proof that you failed. Often, it is the place where God finally dismantles the lie that you were meant to save yourself. That you were meant to be a superhero. That you were meant to do everything yourself, by yourself. There is some unresolved history in all our lives, much we do not know anything about. The iniquity, the sin-debt of ancestors from 500 years ago could be the cause of this siege. Now that we are in Christ, let us lean on the Everlasting Arms. Amen.

Jesus did not come because people were lazy. He came because people were locked in. And once you see that, you stop striving against the siege, and start trusting the Redeemer who already stepped into it.

THE DANGEROUS LIE – GIVE MORE

"Give More to Get Out" is a version of teaching that sounds spiritual but is actually transactional. If you give more, God will move. If you sow more, the siege will lift. If you release something, God will release you. That logic collapses God into a system. It turns trust into leverage, generosity into a bribe, and obedience into a transaction. And under siege, it preys on desperation.

This teaching is especially harmful in a siege is because in a siege, provision is already constrained. Options are already limited. Pressure is already intense To tell someone *"give more"* in that moment subtly implies that y*ou are still in control if you just do the right thing.*

You are not in control in a siege; you are trusting God. Now if God—and you **KNOW** it's God, tells you to give, then by all means do it. But do not be coerced into something that God did not tell you and that bears witness in your spirit man. But siege is defined by the absence of control. This kind of teaching pushes people toward self-rescue, fear-based giving, performance-driven faith, and spiritual bargaining.

That's not faith; that's panic dressed up as obedience.

Scripture does not present giving as a lever. Yes, Scripture teaches generosity, and giving matters. Yes, God honors cheerful, willing hearts, But Scripture does not teach giving to force timing, giving to override governance, or giving to end seasons that God is governing.

Jesus never told besieged people to give more to get out. He told them to trust, follow, wait, remain.

Giving is an act of worship, not a mechanism for escape. Giving flows from trust. It is not used to buy or manufacture outcomes. If God asks someone to give during siege, it will be specific, clear, peaceful, uncoerced, unrushed, and not attached to promises of immediate relief. Anything else is manipulation, even if unintended.

In seasons of siege, people are often told to "give more" in order to force a breakthrough. This teaching mistakes generosity for leverage. Giving is an act of worship, not a tool to escape governance. When God governs a season, no offering can bribe its end. God does not ask for payment; He asks for trust.

Jesus didn't tell the rich young ruler to give his way out of anything or into anything to gain access. No one can buy their way into the Kingdom. Abraham wasn't told to give a tenth. And afterwards the Lord said that Cornelius' gifts had come up as a memorial -- that was free will on the part of Cornelius. There is no man who can say give your way out of anything, even siege, else God would have sent prophets all through the Bible to collect money and that would have made them as tax collectors.

"Give your way out" collapses Biblically. If giving could end sieges, God would have sent prophets to collect money. Instead, He sent prophets to call for repentance, trust, obedience, waiting, and the return of allegiance to God. Not once do we see a prophet in the Bible saying. "Raise an offering and this siege will end." John the Baptist said, Repent, for the Kingdom is at hand. He did not raise an offering. Those who did raise an offering, well it didn't end well. God didn't tell Aaron to collect gold from the Israelites. But he did, and they made a golden calf.

Not just attempting self-rescue – and the Israelites didn't even need to be rescued, they had convinced themselves of false urgency, but they had already turned their backs on God and looking for another idol.

This is so dangerous because in a true siege, options are gone. Power is restrained and self-rescue is actually the temptation. You cannot buy or give your way out of a true siege. That smacks of self-rescue and that functions as invitations to interfere with a process God is governing.

It is not unlike Peter pulling Jesus aside and insisting that He should not be arrested, should not suffer, should not go to the Cross. Peter loved Jesus. His intentions were sincere. But his counsel would have derailed redemption.

Jesus did not rebuke Peter for lack of passion. He rebuked him for misaligned authority.

In the same way, urging action where God has commanded restraint is not faith — it is interference. And interference, even when well-meaning, can oppose what God is accomplishing.

74

"Give more" becomes a false action, a desperate lever, and a way to *feel* obedient while avoiding trust. It is attempting self-rescue, just dressed in church language. No man can give his way out of a siege. The Kingdom of God is not for sale, and God does not fundraise His interventions. Giving is worship, not currency. God cannot be purchased, especially in seasons He Himself governs.

QUICKSAND

Siege behaves like quicksand because of thixotropic pressure. Thixotropic systems resist force but yield to stillness and time. If you have not put your trust in God, and put your hand in His hand, you could be flailing about instead of being still, calm, and trusting Getting through siege successfully is like a dance – how can you both lead? God is the head; He must lead. This is when you finally give your trusts fully over to the Lord and let Him be the Lord. God should be the head of your life, not you. A man cannot have two heads; that is confusion.

Within siege, the harder you struggle, or go against the plan of God, the more resistance increases. Like quicksand, things will tighten up against you and you may find that reaching shore and safety is very difficult to impossible. When the enemy sees you are not settled, you are not one with God, then he keeps piling stuff on. New, sudden, wrong force may lead to deeper entrapment. Panic-driven motion leads to loss of buoyancy. Slow, governed movement results in stabilization and release. That is *exactly* how siege operates.

A siege is not static opposition. Siege is alive and has many moving parts. It is reactive to movements and pressure. When someone under siege pushes harder, rushes decisions, forces outcomes, self-rescues, reacts to pressure, the siege tightens. Not because God punishes effort, but because force is the wrong interaction model. Just like quicksand, vertical thrashing sinks you. Lateral, slow spreading restores flotation. This explains why what *used* to work stops working; some movements are not allowed or authorized right now. Effort produces diminishing returns. Desperation accelerates danger. Stillness becomes safer than action. That is the opposite of how the natural mind is trained.

SCRIPTURES FOR SURVIVAL MODE, STILLNESS, & SIEGE

Stillness as the Antidote to Panic:

Be still, and know that I am God. (Psalms 46:10)

Be still is issued in the context of chaos, not peace. Be still is the spiritual equivalent of *stopping movement in quicksand*. Stillness here means to cease thrashing, stop forcing outcomes, and stop reacting as if God is absent. Why do you cry aloud? Is there no king among you?

God Explicitly Forbids Panic-Based Action

In returning and rest you shall be saved; in quietness and confidence shall be your strength. (Isaiah 30:15)

Siege Language: Stillness While Surrounded.

The LORD will fight for you, and you shall hold your peace. (Exodus 14:14)

Haste as a Spiritual Danger Signal

Whoever believes will not act hastily. (Isaiah 28:16)

Emotional Hijack and Bad Decisions

A man's folly ruins his way, and his heart rages against the LORD. (Proverbs 19:3)

This verse is devastatingly honest. It shows the pattern: Folly (panic decisions). Ruined path. Emotional blame toward God. This is survival mode after the damage is done.

God's Refusal to Lead by Panic

God is not the author of confusion, but of peace. (1 Corinthians 14:33)

Anxiety Shrinking Perspective

Anxiety in a man's heart weighs him d own, but a good word makes him glad. (Proverbs 12:25)

Survival mode is *heavy*. It compresses options. It narrows imagination. It distorts judgment.

Jesus on Divided Attention (Mental Siege)

Martha, Martha, you are anxious and troubled about many things, but one thing is necessary. (Luke 10:41–42)

Anxiety fragments focus. Fragmentation leads to frantic activity. Jesus interrupts it with presence over productivity. This is survival mode corrected by stillness.

The Promise That Stillness Produces Clarity

You will keep him in perfect peace, whose mind is stayed on You. (Isaiah 26:3)

Scripture consistently teaches that panic-based motion degrades discernment. The more the emotional mind hijacks the thinking mind, the more likely destructive decisions become. God's command to "be still" is not spiritual poetry Godly, spiritual intervention. Stillness prevents damage. Haste multiplies it.

Be still, and know that I am God. (Psalm 46:10)

If stillness feels unsafe, or makes you feel anxious or guilty, it is because survival mode is speaking. Scripture does not shame that impulse, it overrides it. That is exactly what survival-mode decisions do in real life. There may come jacked-up offers with bad contracts. Somehow, out of nowhere destructive relationships are offered. Risky "solutions" may be taken. Casino thinking ("maybe this one move will fix it").Scripture warns against this explicitly:

Whoever believes will not act hastily. (Isaiah 28:16)

Haste is a spiritual red flag. Faith is not hasty.

The LORD will fight for you, and you shall hold your peace. (Exodus 14:14)

A siege behaves like quicksand. The more the emotional mind hijacks the intellectual mind, the more frantic movement increases danger. Scripture's command to "be still" is not poetic, it is a protective interruption of survival mode. That sentence is solid theology and solid psychology.

This doesn't mean to "Do nothing forever." It doesn't mean to "Be passive or surrender authority." It says, Change the way you interact with pressure. In siege force is not authority. Motion is not always progress and urgency is not Wisdom. Authority behaves like buoyancy, not propulsion.

Stillness is protective, not passive. In quicksand for example, stillness allows redistribution of pressure. Breath control restores flotation. Slow movements widen surface area. External help becomes possible. Siege really is designed to be a trap, like quicksand. In siege, stillness preserves authority. Restraint prevents bad decisions and shows your alignment with and trust in God. Time reveals manipulation and then Intervention can arrive from outside. the Faith: God will come.

All of the following align with *Stand still and see the salvation of the Lord.* Jericho had six days of silence before the big shout. Dothan's unmoving prophet because he could see that there were more with them than against them. Joseph's unmoving endurance in his first enclosure.

Manipulators rely on reaction, that's why they play a cat-and-mouse game to toy with their would-be victims. Quicksand "wins" when you panic. Manipulation "wins" when you thrash. Stillness removes entertainment. It removes leverage, urgency, and control. The mouse escapes by stopping the game.

A siege is not broken by force. It behaves more like quicksand than a wall. Panic deepens it. Stillness outlasts it.

If you can keep your head when all about you are loosing theirs and blaming it on you. (Rudyard Kipling)

It is hard for you to kick against the goads. (Acts of the Apostles 26:14)

A **goad** was not punishment, it was guidance. It was used to keep an ox aligned and prevent veering into danger. Goads were to correct direction, not crush strength. Kicking against it didn't free the animal, it **injured it**.

In a true siege God restrains movement. God governs timing. God narrows options. The goads are not cruelty. They are containment with intent. To kick against them is to resist restraint, fight guidance and turn pressure into injury.

That's exactly what happens when folks self-rescue and try to force outcomes. It is what happens when people "give" to regain control or act when God has said wait. The pain doesn't come from God, it comes from resisting direction. And I'll say from resisting instruction. When God says be still, then be still.

If siege is a mission, (God's mission, not yours, but you are used in the mission), then the goads define the path. resistance delays arrival, and submission to the mission preserves strength.

Paul wasn't being punished on the road to Damascus. He was being **redirected**. And once he stopped kicking, the mission became clear.

In siege, resistance does not create freedom. It creates wounds. Scripture calls this kicking against the goads. Restraint is not opposition. Sometimes it is direction. If struggling makes it worse, then force is not the answer.

I do not thrash against what tightens under force.
I remain still until the pressure redistributes.

I trust release more than reaction. In the Name of Jesus.
Amen

The more the intellectual mind is hijacked by the emotional mind, the more stupid choices are likely. The more one fidgets and runs around, the worse things can get.

Be still and know I am the Lord.

God says, **Trust Me. Wait. Obey. Remain.** But, not relying—fully relying on God but leaning to one's own understanding is akin to rebellion, disobedience, even witchcraft since rebellion is as the sin of witchcraft. Siege is a SERIOUS, very SERIOUS test. God told Saul to wait for Samuel, but Saul took the act of burning the sacrifice into his own hands, and we know from Scripture that Saul ended up seeking that witch at Endor.

RECOGNIZING THE SIEGE IN SCRIPTURE

One of the most destabilizing aspects of a siege is the feeling that *this should not be happening.*

Scripture does not leave us without precedent—but it does require us to look carefully. Biblical sieges rarely look the way modern believers expect hardship to look. They are often counterintuitive, slow, humbling, and deeply confusing to those inside them.

This chapter exists so you can say, "What I am going through has a name: siege. This has happened to many others before me. God does not hate me. I am not outside the story of God."

Jericho: When Progress Required Stillness. Jericho was not a battle of strength. It was a siege of restraint. The people were armed. They were positioned. They were obedient. And they were told to **wait**, walk, and remain silent. Nothing about that instruction felt strategic. Nothing about it rewarded effort. Nothing about it explained timing.

Jericho teaches this: Sometimes God forbids action precisely because action would steal glory from Divine intervention. The walls did not fall because Israel fought well. They fell because Israel did not interfere. If you are under siege and feel restrained from acting—even wisely—Jericho tells you that restraint can be obedience, not fear.

Samaria: When Conditions Become Absurd. The siege of Samaria was severe, humiliating, and prolonged. Resources disappeared. Normal life collapsed. Logic broke down. Nothing about that siege made sense—not morally, not economically, not spiritually. The people inside could not fix it, pray it away, or strategize their way out.

And then—overnight—conditions reversed.

Scripture records no great action by the people inside the city. Relief came from **outside**, through confusion in the enemy camp. Samaria teaches this: When a siege becomes illogical, its ending will be equally illogical—but in your favor.

If your situation feels unreasonable, disproportionate, or absurd, Samaria says: *you are not imagining this.*

Jerusalem: When Faithfulness Is Still Surrounded. Jerusalem experienced sieges even when kings were faithful and reforms had been made. Siege did not mean God had left. It meant God was working on a national scale, beyond individual righteousness. Jerusalem teaches this: Some sieges are not about personal correction but about larger timing, testimony, and transfer of authority.

If you have searched yourself and found no rebellion—but the pressure remains, Jerusalem tells you that righteousness does not exempt you from enclosure.

Biblical sieges feel familiar although delay does not mean denial. Enclosure does not mean abandonment. Silence does not mean God's absence. Stillness does not mean stagnation.

God ends sieges His way—not ours.

Hold this Truth: You are not experiencing something new. You are experiencing something Biblical. Naming it does not end it—but it steadies you inside it. My situation has precedent. God has ended this before. I am not outside His pattern.

Joseph at Dothan was the first enclosure. *(Genesis 37)* Joseph did not arrive at Dothan by rebellion; he arrived by obedience. He was sent by his father. He was following instruction. He was looking for his brothers. Dothan is where everything collapses. His brothers see him from afar. They conspire; they strip him of his colorful robe and throw him into a well with no water in it. There was no escape; this is Joseph's first siege.

WHEN MINISTRY IS UNDER SIEGE

I've noticed in person and even over the airwaves that A LOT of ministers complain about the sound booth, the microphones, the feedback, the monitors -- anything related to the sound or media ministry. I BELIEVE THE OPPOSITION AGAINST THOSE PEOPLE IS tremendous. It frustrates the speakers/pastors or whatever, but there is real opposition; running the microphones may seem easy, but it depends on what is coming across to be broadcast.

Resistance concentrates when transmission matters. Opposition shows up in sound, media, and transmission. Sound systems, microphones, monitors, livestreams, recordings, even for speakers and pastors who do extensive mic sound checks before the service. These instruments are not neutral accessories; they are the delivery system.

If the message cannot be heard clearly, it does not matter how anointed, prepared, or sincere the speaker is. So, opposition doesn't always aim at the *speaker* directly. It often aims at the channel.

It's the attempt to get in where it can fit in —where there is access. The pastor could be all prayed up. The prayer warrior prophetic intercessor has prayed across the stage for an hour, two hours – has anyone prayed for the media team? Has the media team even prayed for the media team. I'm not saying they haven't, but the warfare is terrific against it and not in a good way. I know this because I've had all kinds of instruments, devices and media glitches that have held up messages, prayers, and uploads for years. I'm prayed up, but my microphone isn't.

The sound/media can be under pressure and disruption. Have you ever noticed that every singer's mic is perfect, but you can barely hear the teacher/speaker/preacher. That's no *coinky-dink* if it happens every service. But then, at least with me, the opposition totally lifts after the service or the message is delivered. Like it never even happened. But it did. This is still a siege and it is aimed at *output*, not *identity*

Ministers get unusually agitated about sound issues. You may have noticed this pattern: Calm before service, Peace during preparation, Then suddenly, as the mic goes live there's feedback, dropouts, echo, distortion, wrong levels, the monitors are not working or tother livestream glitches. The speaker reacts *out of proportion* to the technical issue.

That's not because they're petty. It's because their nervous system knows the transmission is being interfered with. Even if they can't articulate it spiritually, their body registers, "What I'm trying to release is being obstructed And, I've got a mandate to release this word to these people today. Today." That creates frustration, agitation, and sometimes misplaced anger.

This is not "blaming demons for bad tech" This is not excusing or blaming poor preparation. It is not blaming every cable or mixer issue on opposition, it is calling what it is, what it is. If it happens repeatedly, it intensifies at the moment of broadcast, and then resolves afterward and if it it targets sound more than visuals, it's likely a spiritual struggle that needs more prayer because God does want His Word to be made public and broadcast.

Non-media people, perhaps you have occasion to sew or use scissors in your home. Where are those scissors? I don't know about you but I've been sewing since I could thread a needle, but scissors are not where I left them, not where I know they should be – they are the goal of too many scavenger hunts in the same room, on the same table where I know I left them. This is annoyance, a waste of time and once I went out and bought new scissors because I couldn't find the ones I just had in my hand. This is object torment.

Like those scissors, chances are very good that no one did anything to those mics since the last church service, but they are out of whack today for some reason. Well, there's the prince of the powers of the air and he wants to block transmission of the Word of God.

Faith comes by hearing, that sound is very important. Sound penetrates, it bypasses defenses, reaches people who aren't looking, lodges in memory, it lodges in the heart and creates faith and more faith. It shapes belief. Words are alive and they are sent out to accomplish. So, the words are living, moving, being, doing more than a picture or an image, although the eyes are never full.

This is why siege always involves **noise,** such as accusation, repetition. And if it's in your mind and it is a mind-siege with rumination, and worry. Internal or external intimidation, confusion, false testimony can be part of the siege.. The enemy understands sound. He was involved in the worship in Heaven.

And this is why God answers siege not only with action, but with a Word.

Pictures inspire. Images attract. But sound creates faith. Even Scripture acknowledges this limitation of sight:

The eye is not satisfied with seeing. (Ecclesiastes 1:8)

What the eyes cannot hold, the ear can carry. Sound enters where images cannot. Sound remains when images fade. Sound continues working when the siege is still standing. That is why preaching matters. That is why prayer spoken aloud matters. That is why proclamation matters — especially under siege.

Because faith is not born from what we see. Faith is born from what we hear, and what we continue to hear until belief takes root and God acts.

Silencing sound does not require censorship. It only requires distortion. A garbled message is often as effective as no message at all. Opposition prefers *frustration* over silence. Most of the time, the mic doesn't shut off completely. Instead, it squeals, echoes, distracts and breaks concentration. That's intentional in effect, even if the mechanism is natural. The goal is not always to stop the message, sometimes the goal is to fracture the speaker's authority mid-stream.

Frustration breaks flow, especially if the speaker stops for any reason, but especially to scold the media team. The stoppage an disrupt clarity, pulls the speaker out of Presence and weaken or even destroy delivery. This can be without anyone saying a word.

I have more than once experienced intense pressure before and *during* teaching or prayer that lifts immediately afterward. That's my personal version of what happens corporately through sound and media. Same pattern. Same timing. Same release afterward. In both cases access remains. peace returns. the struggle is functional, not personal. the goal is interruption, not destruction.

Speakers and pastors often: lash out at sound teams. Causing them to internalize shame. blame themselves, push harder, or even quit. The speaker then may preach through agitation and this may also distort the spirit of the Word delivered. None of that helps.

And it often turns collaborators into casualties. Sound and media teams are not obstacles — they are front-line participants in transmission. They need to know that and not just think that they are doing the easy job in the church. Back when we were in grade school, the kids who pushed the AV equipment from room to room (when there wasn't enough for each room, but we had to share), maybe they had the easy job because they could leave the classroom, roam the hallways and go into other rooms while the rest of us just sat. This is not that. Media teams behind front-facing ministries need serious prayer, respect, rest, and protection just as much as the person holding the mic.

When Truth is meant to be transmitted, resistance often targets the channel rather than the source. This is why sound and media ministries experience disproportionate pressure at the moment of broadcast. Distortion accomplishes what silence cannot do. It disrupts authority without openly opposing it.

The Wisdom response is not yelling at the sound booth or media team. It's not pushing harder. It's not spiritual theatrics. It's calm authority, patience, slowing the moment, maintaining presence, blessing the channel, refusing agitation. Stillness stabilizes transmission. That's true spiritually *and* technically. Opposition against sound is not a compliment. It's not proof of greatness. It's simply a sign that what is being carried matters. And the correct response is not pressure. It's governed peace.

What covenants are governing you not because you chose them, but because you were born into them? Which ones have already been answered by Christ—and which ones are still operating because no one has named them? That's discernment based.

A siege often isn't random; instead, it's a covenantal pressure point. A line being contested, An inheritance being resisted, A permission being challenged. Sometimes the siege lifts not because you fought harder, but because you finally understood what you were standing for.

But I say, Have they not heard? Yes verily, their sound went into all the earth, and their words unto the ends of the world. (Romans 10:18)

THE RESTORATION OF AUTHORITY

A siege does not end with relief alone. It ends with authority being restored and with you returning to circulation.

This is important, because many people mistake relief for restoration. They feel pressure lift and assume everything is complete—only to discover later that they hesitate, second-guess, or move tentatively, unsure whether they are truly free. Authority answers that uncertainty.

Authority is not given back; it is released. Authority is not lost in a siege. It is held in reserve. During containment, authority is restrained not because it is dangerous—but because it would be misused under pressure. Authority exercised too early would become self-rescue. It would turn trust into control.

So, God guards it.

When the siege lifts, authority does not need rebuilding, requalifying, or proving. It simply returns to use. This is why restored authority often feels quiet rather than dramatic.

Authority returns in recognizable ways: You stop asking permission for things you are already allowed to do. You move without rehearsing outcomes. You decide without panic. You speak without needing validation. You act without rushing. This is not boldness. It is governance. Authority does not announce itself. It operates.

Before a siege, authority often feels energetic. After a siege, authority feels settled. You are no longer proving faith. You are no longer negotiating trust. You are no longer forcing outcomes. You know what you can do—and what you do not need to do. This is maturity forged under restraint.

This marks the end of over-explaining, as one of the first signs of restored authority is silence. Not withdrawal, secrecy. But the end of explaining yourself. You no longer feel compelled to justify delays, Defend obedience. Clarify misunderstood seasons, prove faithfulness. Authority does not narrate itself.

God restores authority before momentum because momentum without authority recreates chaos. So God restores authority first. That is why opportunities may come slowly at first. Movement may feel measured. Doors open without pressure to rush through them. Authority sets pace; momentum follows later.

The Difference Between Power and Authority (Revisited) is that power demands movement, while authority permits it. Power reacts. Authority governs. Authority cannot be fully restored until the siege is understood.

After a siege, God does not give you power back. He gives you permission to move again—without anxiety.

Do Not Shrink After Authority Returns. Some people stay small because they fear losing freedom again. But authority restored is not fragile. You do not need to tiptoe. You do not need to ask, "Is this okay?" You do not need to relive the siege to stay humble.

Humility is already built in.

Hold this Truth: You did not survive the siege to remain cautious forever. You were preserved so that when authority returned, it would be exercised cleanly.

Authority has returned to my life.
I move without haste and without fear.
I govern what God has entrusted to me.

GET-OUT-OF-SIEGE PRAYERS

These are not spiritual warfare prayers. They are not shouted. They do not rebuke enemies. They do not force outcomes. They are alignment prayers—spoken from inside containment, not from panic.

Prayer 1: Acknowledging the Siege

Father,
I stop pretending this is something else.
I acknowledge that I am enclosed, not abandoned.
I release the need to explain this season.
I accept that this is not corrected by effort.
I remain where You have kept me,
without accusing myself,
and without accusing You. In the Name of Jesus. Amen.

Prayer 2: Renouncing Self-Rescue

Father,
I release every plan born from pressure.
I renounce premature exits and forced solutions.
I refuse to trade alignment for relief.

I lay down the need to make something happen.
I trust You more than I trust momentum. In the Name of
Jesus. Amen.

Prayer 3: Guarding the Well

Father God,
I return to You without agenda.
I stop demanding answers in place of presence.
I protect my access to You from anxiety, striving, and noise.
Let my well remain clean while I wait. In the Name of
Jesus. Amen.

Prayer 4: Waiting Without Withering

Father God,
I ask not for escape, but for preservation.
Keep me whole while I remain.
Let this season not reduce me,
but refine me.
I choose endurance without self-abandonment.

Prayer 5: Readiness for Relief

Father God,
I trust that relief will come from outside this season.
I will recognize it when it arrives.
I will not miss it by forcing my own exit.
Prepare me to move when You lift restraint. In the Name of
Jesus. Amen.

Prayer 6: Authority Re-Engagement

Father,
As restraint lifts,
I receive restored authority without fear.
I move forward without rushing,
and without shrinking.
I step into what You now permit. In the Name of Jesus.
Amen.

Final Still Prayer (No Asking)

Father God,
I am here.
I remain.
I trust You.

NEVER MAKE A LIFE-CHANGING DECISION WHILE UNDER SIEGE

A siege does not just restrict movement, it can also distort judgment. This is one of the most dangerous truths about siege seasons. Under siege, your brain is trying to escape pressure, choose wisely, and it thinks it is saving your life. Moment by moment. That does not make you foolish. It makes you human under prolonged constraint.

Siege decisions feel urgent because siege creates *false life or death urgency*. The pressure builds quietly until relief feels more important than alignment. At that point, decisions are no longer evaluated by Wisdom, but by how quickly they promise change. This is how people under siege see and say things differently than they normally would. If you have a friend that is full of drama, they may be in survival mode, under siege, or even under witchcraft attack which brings on the exact response as survival mode. Of course I'll say more here. Recall at the beginning of this book I said that you've done the work already and that may be why you are surprised to be under siege. Part of the work was to find out what's going on spiritually around you. How did you get here? You may not be able to articulate it, but you can still know it. You asked God if you were under judgment, right? And He said you were not. Perfect.

You then asked if these delays, obstacles, hindrances, embargos and being boxed in was a result of witchcraft attack or some other occultic mechanism against you. Right? You did that, *right*? So, you already knew and you had already prayed your warfare and other prayers against these attacks to include fasting? Well done. The oppression let up and you were thankful.

However, some of these evil agent types don't stop. They may pretend to stop, but when an evil altar has been fired up against you, it's going to take a greater altar to stop it. God hears your prayers and answers. Amen. So the evil agents of the enemy backed off. But why and how are you under siege now? Well, that's where God comes in; He has a purpose in all of this. If God is allowing a thing, He is using it.

Now, hopefully you didn't take any shortcuts to get past the spiritual attacks that were coming at you. Hopefully you didn't just try to stop the symptoms so you could feel better, get some sleep at night and continue to push forward, leaning on your own understanding. You didn't think that: "At least something would be different."

- "I can't stay here forever."

- "This is better than nothing."

- "God understands why I'd do this."

That last sentence is the most dangerous one.

Temporary relief can mask a permanent trap. Siege decisions often work—briefly. Some people just want to make it through today and let tomorrow worry about tomorrow. That's why these traps are so deceptive.

- The money hits the account

- The relationship dulls the loneliness

- The move breaks the pressure

- The risk produces a rush of hope

- Or it dulls the senses, so a person forgets their problems—for the time being.

Oh, so you didn't do the work correctly and now you're in dire straits: siege. That explains a lot. For a moment, the oppression feels lighter but now a whole siege is in place. Within the siege, you could make decisions for temporary fixes, but, they often damage permanently. Because the decision was never meant to build a future—only to end discomfort. Symptoms, not solutions.

Desperation masquerades as opportunity in spiritual matters. Under attack or siege, bad options don't look bad. They look timely, Convenient, available, "God-sent," or like a door opening. It's why we need discernment big time to know the difference between temptation and opportunity.

Availability is not authorization--, did God say do that? Did God say it was okay to do that? Some of the most destructive choices in Scripture were *available*—they were just made under pressure, hunger, fear, or fatigue.

For example, a person under siege financially may realize they have no money. The wise response would be to budget, ask for help, wait, preserve, A siege-distorted response says, "I might as well try something." So, they go to a casino.

Why?

Because desperation reframes risk as hope. And even if they win once, the pattern is established. Now they think they can solve financial pressure by gambling. Even after the siege ends, the habit can remain.

Never make a life-changing or permanent decision while under siege. Never make a life-changing or permanent decision while in survival mode. Never make a life-changing or permanent decision while under witchcraft attack.

No marriage, divorce, having kids, relocation, major financial commitments, career decisions, especially abandonment. Do not go into risky investments or make any covenant-breaking choices. Do not take on temporary solutions that have lasting consequences. Sieges end. Permanent decisions do not reverse easily.

THE SIEGE DECISION CHECKLIST

Before making any major decision, ask:

1. Would I choose this if I weren't desperate?

If the honest answer is *no*, stop.

2. Does this decision promise fast relief but long-term cost?

Fast relief + long-term sacrifice = siege trap.

3. Is this reversible?

Never make irreversible decisions under reversible pressure.

4. Am I thinking in extremes?

Siege thinking says:

- "Anything is better than this."
- "I have no other options. Extreme thinking is a warning sign.

5. Have I invited at least one calm, non-urgent voice into this decision?

Siege isolates. Wisdom requires witness.

6. If it requires you to become someone you don't recognize, it's not Wisdom.

7. Does peace come *after* the decision—or only *because* pressure stops? True peace does not depend on escape.

Instead, when the urge to self-solve hits, delay the decision. Reduce exposure to temptation. Narrow your world temporarily. Guard the well. Let pressure pass without acting on it.

Doing nothing is often the most faithful move in a siege.

Life is not about perfection. You are not failing because you feel tempted to self-solve. The victory is not *never feeling desperation*. The victory is not letting desperation govern authority.

Hold this Truth: A siege is not the season to fix your life; it is the season to preserve your future.

Father God,
I refuse to trade my future for relief.
I choose preservation over panic.
Keep me from decisions I would regret
once this pressure lifts. In the Name of Jesus. Amen.

WHEN PEOPLE WHO HELP CREATE THE SIEGE OFFER TO SAVE YOU

One of the most confusing aspects of a siege is this: The very people, systems, or circumstances that contributed to the enclosure often reappear as the proposed solution. This does not happen accidentally. And it does not mean they are evil caricatures. But don't deceive yourself, sometimes they are evil characters; discern every *spirit*. Pressure creates leverage—and leverage seeks an outlet. Evil folks would love to capitalize on the downfall that they hope you are about to experience.

But God is coming! You don't have to tell them that, just know it. Hold to that Truth.

Siege pressure is applied through people. However, not all sieges come from enemies you can identify. Many come through authority structures, relationships, institutions, gatekeepers, family dynamics, economic dependencies, and other "necessary" systems. These pressures may not be malicious at first. Sometimes they begin as constraints, expectations, or control justified as wisdom, help, or responsibility.

Over time, however, the effect is the same. You may feel trapped, limited, unable to move freely, dependent on forces outside your control. That is siege.

When desperation peaks, something predictable happens. The same source of pressure suddenly offers relief and that is at the worst moment. It may sound like, "I can help you out of this…" "If you'd just agree to this one thing…" "This wouldn't be happening if you'd listened earlier." "Let me fix this for you." The offer often comes just before you would have been able to endure without it.

Timing matters.

The hidden goal: desperation-driven compliance. Siege pressure does not always aim to destroy you, often, it aims to reshape you, to own you, to make you beholding to them. The goal is not your collapse, but your consent. When people or systems apply pressure long enough, they expect you to lower boundaries, accept inferior terms, trade autonomy for relief, relinquish authority "temporarily." Agree to conditions you would never accept at Peace; sometimes it is an initiation.

Desperation becomes the negotiating tool. Many times it is during a fast or at the end of a consecration, the enemy wants to re-enlist you from something you just broke spiritually free from.

It can feel like salvation or deliverance. This is so dangerous because relief offered by the source of pressure feels *powerful*. It works. It changes circumstances. It ends discomfort. It restores movement--, well, for a moment. It could very well form an alliance or an initiation that you were not planning for. Especially when that relief requires submission, silence, or dependency is not deliverance. It is containment with your own permission.

A critical discernment question is: "Does this help restore my authority—or replace it?"

True help strengthens agency, preserves dignity, restores autonomy. It does not require silence or indebtedness. While false rescue requires compliance, demands gratitude under pressure, rewrites the narrative of how you got here, and positions the helper as essential.

Consider the character of the person you are dealing with. I know a man that if he does anything for you, any little thing at all, you will NEVER pay him back. He will NEVER let you forget it. If that is the type of character who wants to rescue you, let that boat pass and wait on the Lord. Again, I say, wait.

God allows this moment at a crossroads because authority must be chosen, not just restored. If you accept rescue that costs authority, you exit the siege physically but remain enclosed spiritually. The pressure lifts—but governance does not return. That's why some people escape one siege only to enter another.

Joseph, Dothan, and false rescues: Joseph's brothers caused his enclosure. They did not rescue him. Potiphar's house looked like rescue; but it was positioning. Prison looked like regression; it was protection. God's deliverance did not come through those who caused the harm—or those who benefited from it—but through timing that restored Joseph's authority without indebtedness.

That pattern repeats.

Know how to recognize a siege-based trap. Be cautious if the "rescue" requires urgency, silence, or loyalty under pressure. Guard yourself if it reframes your memory of the siege. If it makes you feel small for needing help, it's demeaning and that is not God. If it positions someone else as indispensable it's most likely a trap. Especially if the offer comes with words like, "This is the only way." God rarely rescues people through ultimatums.

If a moment like this comes, do not decide immediately. Pressure-based help collapses when delayed. Look, see, and name the source of the pressure honestly. Without accusation—just clarity. Ask what the help costs long-term, not what it fixes short-term. Protect your authority even if you stay uncomfortable longer.

Endurance is sometimes safer than relief.

Hold this Truth: Not every open hand is deliverance. Some are leverage waiting for desperation. You may have to decide and say, If I perish, I perish, but I will not enter or re-enter into and evil covenant, alliance or deal with the dark kingdom or any of its representatives. And, Amen.

If the same source that applied pressure now offers relief, slow down. No, STOP. God's rescue does not require you to surrender the very authority He intends to restore.

Pray this: I will not let desperation decide who governs my life. I wait for relief that restores, not replaces, my authority.

REFUSING TO BE TOYED WITH

One of the most degrading experiences in a siege is the sense of being toyed with. Not attacked outright. Not destroyed, but provoked, delayed, dangled, pressured, and manipulated just enough to keep you reacting.

This is not imagination. This is not hypersensitivity. This is a known spiritual pattern. And, even if you don't have words for it, you still know. If you know, you know that there is some spiritual manipulation going on here. There are some cat-and-mouse dynamics going on.

Being "Toyed With" means someone controls your access, timing, or relief. Pressure is applied, then withdrawn, then reapplied. Hope is dangled, then delayed. Help is offered conditionally. Silence is used strategically. Your reactions are being measured.

The goal is to keep you reactive and defensive instead of authoritative. A reactive person can be steered. An authoritative person cannot.

Sieges create vulnerability by inviting cat-and-mouse behaviors. When movement is restricted and pressure is sustained, people naturally seek signals, they look for openings. The respond to cues and can over-interpret changes. This heightened sensitivity makes them easier to manipulate.

Cat-and-mouse dynamics feed on attention and reaction, not strength. That's why the mouse isn't chased constantly. It's released… then pursued… then watched.

Reaction is the reward.

There is spiritual danger in constant reactions. Reaction erodes authority quietly. When you are reacting, you are explaining instead of governing. You are responding instead of deciding. You are adjusting instead of standing. You are tracking others instead of discerning God. Reaction keeps you off center.

And anything that keeps you off center can toy with you.

End spiritual toying. The hard but freeing truth: Toying ends when reaction ends. Not when confrontation happens. Not when explanations are given. Not when demands are made. But when access to your emotional and decisional center is withdrawn.

In Scripture, the enemy loses power when access is denied, not when force is applied.

The shift from mouse to witness is the turning point. You stop being the mouse when you stop running patterns. That looks like when you keep a cooler head and are no longer responding immediately or frantically. You are no longer explaining yourself. Least of all are you expecting clarity from the actual source of pressure. You ae no longer reacting to provocation. No longer adjusting posture based on others' moves. They say jump, you don't say "How high?" You don't even jump anymore.

You become still. You are at Peace; you are at rest in the Everlasting Arms. Stillness is not passivity. Stillness is governed presence.

Stillness breaks the game because cat-and-mouse requires movement. When the mouse stops reacting, the game loses purpose. The manipulator is exposed. Pressure loses leverage. Timing collapses. Stillness removes entertainment value. Stillness removes leverage. Stillness restores authority. This is why Scripture says. *"Stand still and see the salvation of the Lord."* Do not run. Do not argue. Do not fix anything.

Stand.

For spiritual protection from being toyed with do the following. This protection is not mystical. It is positional. Reduce access. Not everyone deserves your response, update, or reaction. Slow your timing. Urgency feeds manipulation. Delay starves the game. Stop explaining; explanation gives manipulators data. Anchor yourself to the Lord. Let your anchors be internal. Return your authority inward to God, not tied to circumstances. Refuse emotional bait. Provocation only works if you bite.

You know the protection is working when you notice less compulsion to respond. Its working because now you have less emotional fluctuations. You have less need to prove or defend; instead, you have more clarity, more Peace, and more silence.

Even as others become louder or quieter, you will remain steadier. That is authority reasserting itself.

This is not withdrawal; it is governance. You are not hiding, retreating, or disengaging from life. You are removing yourself from the game. Games cannot continue without players.

Hold this Truth: You are not here to be managed, tested, dangled, or toyed with. You are here to govern what God has entrusted to you.

Prayer

Father God,
I withdraw my reactions.
I reclaim my center.
I refuse to be moved by manipulation.
I stand where You have placed me.
I am not prey. In the Name of Jesus. Amen.

A PROPHETIC WORD

There are moments when a prophetic declaration ends a siege.

He sent His Word and healed them. (Psalms 107:20)

To declare an end to a siege of any kind the Word spoken has to be sent from the Lord. That sent Word is sent by someone with the gift of prophecy, or by someone who occupies the office of Prophet. However it is sent, there is time that you or the person under siege must agree with Heaven regarding the ending, the lifting of a siege.

This is not *I-wish,* or just because you want it to be over. Of course you want stagnation to be over, but most people attempt it at the wrong time, from the wrong posture, and for the wrong reason. And are they sent by God for this purpose?

Siege produces a "cabin fever" and near-breakdown. Siege pressure doesn't just restrict movement; it compresses the psyche. Over time, people experience loss of perceived control, agitation without cause, a sense of being "about to snap," impulsive urges ("I just need to DO something"), temptation to abandon everything. This is not rebellion; it is nervous system overload under sustained restraint. Scripture recognizes this state and *never* commands people to explode out of it. Instead, God repeatedly interrupts motion before He restores movement.

The dangerous misunderstanding about prophetic declarations is that many people are taught that if you just declare hard enough, long enough, loud enough — it will end. That could be true if you're a real prophet and authorized to make that declaration. It could be true if you have received a Word from the Lord or from a prophet that is anointed of God with that *sent* Word.

Simplifying that teaching causes harm in siege seasons. Because authority is not volume or decibel level, and declaration is not incantation. Trying to "end" a siege prematurely with declarations, especially unsanctioned declarations can deepen frustration, increase self-blame ("Why didn't it work?"), provoke panic, harden desperation, and trigger more self-rescue behavior. In other words, a declaration spoken from survival mode does not carry governing authority.

A prophetic declaration is NOT appropriate, and it does not end a siege when it is motivated by desperation. Or, it is simply to make the pain or discomfort stop. it is driven by agitation or fear, used to override timing, or it is meant to force God's hand or to replace endurance with demand. In Scripture, declarations spoken in panic usually end in regret, not deliverance.

A siege ends when authority re-engages, not when pressure peaks. For the person or people in siege, every day is a pressure peak. A prophetic declaration is appropriate only when stillness has already returned. Now, your trust is fully in the Lord, and His process. No frantic energy. No emotional flooding. No urgency driving speech. Self-rescue has been renounced; You are not trying to escape. You are not bargaining, trying to make a deal with God. You are not threatening God with collapse, or some other vain threat. The declaration is confirmatory, not coercive. You are naming what has already shifted. You are not trying to force the shift.

Fully putting your trust in the Lord, your words and prayers are simple. No long, shouting, striving prayers. Instead, the declaration carries peace, not adrenaline. Authority feels calm, It is neither charged, nor dramatic.

In Scripture, when deliverance is declared *correctly*, it is often brief. Sometimes it is only one word, Rise. Other Biblical declarations that ended sieges are:

- "Stand still."

- **"It is finished."**

- "Let my people go."

- "Today this Scripture is fulfilled."

What a true siege-ending declaration sounds like is not, "I declare this siege is over right now!" But something closer to, "This restraint has completed its work." Or, "I receive the release that has already been prepared." Or even, "I step into what You now permit." The prophetic end to sieges is often spoken calmly. Not always, but most often.

If you feel frantic, pressured, or on the verge of breaking, that is not the moment to declare. That is the moment to be still and make sure you are in the will of God and trusting His plan and purpose for the siege. (If God is allowing a thing, He is using it.)

I will not destroy myself trying to end what God is completing.

Without faith, it is impossible to please God. When you are in faith, you are not in desperation; therefore, you are in line to receive that healing Word from the Lord.

That's Mercy.

When Joshua and all that were with him marched around the walls of Jericho for six days, that was the same number of days that it took to Create the Heavens and the Earth. Faith. It was not until the seventh day that they entered into the "rest" of God, and that is a rest from siege.

JESUS *WITHIN* THE SIEGE

Jesus did not merely experience pressure; He entered a complete siege system so we would never have to be trapped in one without hope. He was surrounded by religious authority, constrained by political power, misjudged by the people, accused by spiritual forces, abandoned relationally, and silenced procedurally. **But He did not rescue Himself**. Not because He could not. He certainly could have, but *self-rescue would have broken the plan*. Jesus could have called more than twelve legions of Angels.

Self-rescue or attempts at self-rescue is like declaring one's own glory-- essentially. For the man who glorifies himself, it is no glory at all. Instead, Jesus chose restraint so **GOD** could act once, fully, and forever.

The siege that Jesus endured guarantees ours will end. Jesus did not just endure siege, He absorbed it. He endured every system that traps people, from accusation to delay, condemnation, power. Imbalance, false judgment. Even spiritual foreclosure was allowed to close in on Him.

Then God did what He always does when fullness is complete. He acted.

The Resurrection did not rush the Cross, and the Cross did not cancel the RESURRECTION.

Jesus was besieged on every side. There was existing religious authority, political power, public opinion, and spiritual opposition. Jesus did not resist. He did not explain. He did not call Angels.

Why?

Because redemption required that GOD do everything.

In a very real sense, the Cross was a table. The Cross was a threshing floor.

The Cross was an altar.

Jesus was full under siege -- Pharisees, Romans, Sanhedrin, the people, the devil. He did more than any one or any group of us ever could, and He let God be God. God did everything there. Count it to your credit when God uses you in this way. If God sends you or allows a very specific mission to happen because of you and using you (you're not directing the mission, God is), that means that He trusts that you won't mess up His plan, even if you don't fully know His plan. Sometimes in siege the plan is not fully known until siege is completely over.

Jesus was not briefly pressured; He was comprehensively besieged. Religious authority (Pharisees, scribes, Sanhedrin), political power (Rome, Pilate, Herod). Public opinion (the crowd that turned on Him. Spiritual opposition (temptation, accusation, silence). Relational abandonment (betrayal, denial, scattering). Nothing about the Cross was accidental. And nothing about it was *rescued* by human initiative.

Jesus did not end the siege, He *entered* it

Jesus did not expose every enemy. He did not call Angels (though He could have). He didn't correct every false charge; He was mostly silent. He didn't clarify every misunderstanding. He didn't preserve His reputation. He allowed the siege to fully form and run its course.

Why?

Because Redemption required silence instead of defense. It required restraint instead of resistance. It required trust instead of explanation.

He was oppressed and afflicted, yet He opened not His
mouth. (Isaiah 53:7)

That is not weakness. That is perfect obedience under total siege.

God did everything there. Yes, that is the point. The Cross is the ultimate proof that Salvation is not collaborative. Redemption is not co-authored. rescue is not negotiated. Jesus did not help God save the world.

He submitted Himself so God could act without interference. That's why the resurrection came from outside the system. No human hand raised Him. No Disciple assisted. No Angel was requested. God acted alone.

When God uses someone this way it means that He trusts that you won't mess up His plan, even if you don't fully know His plan. That's faith. That's trust. That's obedience. That's relationship. Jesus said we should come into the Kingdom as a little child. That is a child taking his parent's hand to cross a busy street to the *other side – no question. Just do it.*

When God allows someone to remain under siege without explanation, it is not because He hates them or they are unimportant or expendable. They are not being punished. It is because interference would damage the outcome. Premature action would corrupt the plan. Silence is required for completion. That kind of trust is not given lightly. It is given to those who will not panic, will not self-vindicate, will not force clarity, will not take shortcuts (even if they've done it in the past—but now they've learned better.) And that besieged person will not seize control (or try to).

This reframes suffering without glorifying it. This is important. When God assumes full responsibility for the outcome, He often removes the illusion that we are needed to manage it.

Jesus' role was not to *solve* the siege. It was to remain obedient inside it. That obedience made redemption possible.

Jesus was besieged on every side, yet He did not intervene, retaliate, or escape. Redemption required that God do everything—and that the Son not interfere with the plan He trusted the Father to complete. When God entrusts someone with silence under siege, it is not abandonment. It is assignment.

Jesus proves forever that siege does not mean God has lost control. Silence does not mean God is absent. Waiting does not mean God is unsure: sometimes He is waiting on us. Sometimes He is waiting for the iniquity of the enemies and for them to gather. In my case He will either prepare a table before me, or a threshing floor for me to arise and thresh. Or, maybe both.

Sometimes God's highest work requires that we do not touch it.

And when He uses someone that way, yes — it is counted to their credit. Not because they understood everything. But because they trusted Him not to fail. God is never plan-less. Scripture is unambiguous about this.

Known unto God are all His works from the beginning of the world. (Acts 15:18)

A siege does not mean God is improvising. Silence does not mean God is reconsidering. Delay does not mean God is unsure. Planlessness is a human condition — not a divine one. When Scripture shows God waiting, it is never because He is undecided. It is because timing is integral to justice. Fullness must be completed. witnesses must be established. The outcome must be irreversible.

That's why Jesus could remain silent under total siege. He wasn't guessing what would happen next. He was trusting a plan already settled. God does not wait because He lacks a plan. He waits because the plan requires time to mature. What looks like uncertainty to us is often precision to God.

And the separation that happened there was final.

This book has never been about predicting how God will end a siege. It is about recognizing when the moment has arrived, and how to stand when it has. A siege does not mean God has lost control it means the field has been set. Did God ever lose control of Jesus on the Cross? Does He not say that His eye is even on the sparrow? Then you should never think that God has lost your location or doesn't have knowledge or power over what is happening to you right not. Even, right now.

The table is prepared. The threshing floor is ready. Jesus has already taken and defeated the Cross, so you or I don't have to. So that leaves the table while we wait out this siege or we are to arise and thresh because of the enemies that have gathered. The only question is this: Has God told you to sit, or to arise?

That timing is the proof.

We know God is coming, not because we feel it, not because pressure increases, and not just because enemies gather. We know because Jesus entered siege intentionally. Jesus did not self-rescue. Jesus trusted the Father's timing. Jesus rose when the plan was complete. So now, for those who are in Christ, siege is never permanent. God's seeming silence is never abandonment. Waiting is never wasted. And, pressure is never final.

God may not come when we want. But because of the Cross, He will come, and He will always come *on time*.

Jesus entered the siege system and was crucified within it, so that no siege we face can end without resurrection. Because Jesus was besieged and raised, siege no longer has the final word.

He will come. Not on our clock. But always on time.

He prepares a table. This time, a communion table. The table has always been more than a place of comfort. In Scripture, the altar, the threshing floor, and the table are not separate ideas; they are stages of the same work.

At the altar, something is offered. At the threshing floor, the wheat is separated from chaff. At the table, what remains is given.

David prepared an altar on a threshing floor. Grain was beaten there before it ever became bread. And bread, once broken, becomes provision. Jesus did not invite His Disciples to a battlefield; He invited them to a table. But it was a table that came after pressure, after betrayal was named, and after sifting had already begun. Jesus was scourged, but we now know Him as Bread of Heaven.

He is the Bread and His Blood is the wine. He has set a communion table for us. This is not denial of the threshing; it is the fruit of it. What survives the pressure is what is shared. What endures the sifting becomes nourishment. What is broken rightly becomes life. So, when Jesus prepares a table, He is not pretending the siege never happened. He is declaring that the work is complete. **It is Finished,** and what remains is enough.

THE SUDDENLY OF GOD

Siege often ends with a *Suddenly of God* Not gradually, Not incrementally, NOT Even explainably—you wake up one day and it just *is*. Just like waking up one morning to 3 feet of snow and it wasn't even snowing last night, or you wake up and all the snow that was there is gone. Overnight.

Suddenlies are not chaos. They are the unveiling of a decision already made. They are the reveal of what God was planning and doing all along.

A suddenly is not God changing His mind or God reacting late. It is not God improvising or being coerced into anything. A suddenly is What it looks like when God moves without resistance. We know this because in Genesis, God spoke and things immediately fell into alignment and into place. How many of us can create what God created in a day? Just one day.

For a long time, something was *restrained*—whether authority, timing, permission, or alignment. But, when restraint lifts, movement looks instant, but it isn't new.

Siege-release feels invisible. From the human side it looks like nothing has changed. There was no warning or signal, necessarily. From God's side, from the Divine side, resistance has ended, interference has ceased, timing is now aligned, and permission was released. It's like the siege broke and more like the siege expired. But really, a siege must be lifted and from an external source. When all that has happened, that's why it feels so quiet.

No human wouldn't embrace the end to a siege whether it came with quiet or if it came with a marching band parade.

Let's look at some versions of sieges that are more dramatic. Namely, the "last-minute breakthrough." I think too many of us are used to those, or we wish for those or desperately need those. Breakthroughs don't happen at the last minute because **God** procrastinated. They happen because a lot of the time, you have too many folks involved in your siege. Do you have too many people involved in your personal business? Does everybody know what you're going through and you're asking everybody you are kin to and friends with to help you? This all could lead to human interference and hey – as long as **you've** got this, why should God be doing anything for you? You didn't like God's timing? So, you strive to "fix it" yourself or get your family and friends to help you fix the problem(s). Okay then.

(You know another siege will be slated for you. Another one will come around until you learn to lean on God.)

God's timing is exact. Human obedience is not. So, when everything *finally* lines up, it feels dramatic, but it's actually order restored. And maybe it came through at the last possible moment.

Worse, is the person who keeps getting in God's way and they keep experiencing disappointment at the edge of breakthrough. That's a real thing.

Sometimes a door or window opens, and you can see the solution is right there. Alignment is near. Release seems imminent, but something happens. Something always happens. Now we can pray to break that power, *spirit* or phenomenon, but we also have to do something ourselves, about ourselves.

If we are so desperate for this breakthrough, or we have experienced so many losses before, we may be emotionally conditioned into fear. When fear speaks it may get you to do something that is not conducive to a Godly finish of this would-be breakthrough. If we try to grab control, or we invite a lot of "help" from people into the dynamic, then that's self-rescue and God is blocked. That doesn't mean God failed. It means that interference can postpone what was ready to be revealed.

Hey, I'm just naming the pattern.

God often ends sieges without warning. There is no announcement. No countdown. No visible transition. One day the pressure is there, then the next day, it isn't. This is release. Suddenlies are not reactions. They are the visible moment when restraint lifts.

When interference ends, movement appears instantly. This is why breakthroughs feel last-minute — as if God arrived in the 11th hour. For all we know, we could have messed up so bad that the Mercy of God had to kick in to get us out of a pickle and then He may also have said, I'll give them a do-over later. Are we taking the same test over and over? Maybe Mercy is 11th hour and you were in the way the entire time?

God is not late, but resistance finally ceased.

Disappointment can occur at the edge of breakthrough — not because God withdrew, but because human intervention reintroduced friction where trust was required. God's suddenlies do not reward effort. They reveal alignment. And when they come, they rarely explain themselves. They simply *are*.

GOD IS COMING

Siege is like a final "season" exam, albeit open book, open Heaven. God's open Hand and His Grace are offered. But it is an exam and exams are not for punishment; they are for promotion. An exam is not a surprise punishment in place to shame anyone. It is necessary as proof of instruction and mastery. It is usually for the purpose of promotion. Testing preceded entrustment. Proving precedes authority. Refinement precedes responsibility. Well, Amen.

An exam reveals readiness.

Siege is not punishment. It is examination—and examinations are given because promotion is possible, or even nearby.

Power belongs to God. If you know that in a season of siege, then you know everything. If you can rest on that knowledge, then you are resting in the Lord. When all barrels of the enemy are pointed at you, then you must say, Lord, I believe You. I trust You. I know you will deliver. You were in the fiery furnace with the Hebrew boys. You were in the lion's den. You got Joseph out of that well. You got Joseph out of the grips of Potiphar's wife who wanted his virtues, you got Joseph out of the prison, you brought millions over the Red Sea on dry land. You pulled down the walls of Jericho. You kept many alive in the famine by the hand of Your steward, Joseph, You redeemed mankind from death, hell, destruction and the grave. There is nothing that You cannot do. You saved David-- how many times from Saul and even from his own sons. You kept mankind alive in the flood. You are God and there is none like You There is none greater than You. And even though they may arise, Lord, Jehovah Sa'ba'oth, you will defeat them, every time. And, Amen.

The iniquity of the Amorites is not yet full.
(Genesis 15:16)

The above sentence is devastatingly sober. It means that God already knew the outcome. God already held the land in promise. God already possessed the power to act. Yet He restrained action until fullness occurred, because God does not judge prematurely. He does not intervene halfway. He does not act on partial evidence. When God moves, it is complete, justified, and irreversible.

Fullness is not just moral wickedness; it is exposure without excuse. Iniquity becomes "full" when repentance is refused, restraint is rejected, warning is ignored, patterns harden, truth is resisted repeatedly. At that point, delay is no longer Mercy; it becomes confirmation.

And when God acts after *fullness*, no one can say, "This wasn't fair." "This wasn't deserved." "This was too much."

From inside a siege, it feels like God is waiting or that God is slow, silent, or not paying attention. Scripture shows that God is often waiting for *them*, not for you. He is

128

waiting for exposure to complete itself. Waiting for self-deception to collapse. Or waiting for alliances to reveal themselves or for intent to become unmistakable. This is why sieges sometimes feel *unnecessarily long.*

But has the Lord not set a table before you, even in the midst of all these seeming delays? They are not about endurance only. They are about witness and your side, they are about trusting the Lord, and they are about patience.

Power never leaves God's hands. NEVER. Power still belongs to our God. Always. God's restraint is not weakness. It is authority under control. If God lacked power, He would need to act immediately. Because God has power, He can afford to wait.

Dangerously, people under siege often assume that if God hasn't acted, that they must. Best to ask God, if He is waiting on you. He will tell you, if you ask Him. But most often, He is not; He is waiting on iniquity of the oppressors to be full. Or, God is waiting for them all to gather. All of them. When God is waiting for iniquity to be full, unauthorized human action interrupts justice. Forced outcomes are temporary and seen as an attempt to steal God's Glory. Self-rescue is interference and creates liability

Waiting, in cases like this, is not passivity. It is alignment with timing that is larger than you.

God's delay is not the absence of power, but the discipline of it. Power belongs to God — and He knows when it must be released. When God waits, it's because He is a Finisher. When He acts, the matter is done and dusted.

Power belongs to God. Timing belongs to God. Judgment belongs to God. Rescue and resolution of siege belong to God. Our role under siege is not to force timing, but to remain aligned until fullness speaks for itself.

All power still belongs to our God.

There are moments in siege when the question is not *whether* God has power, but why He is not yet using it. Sometimes He is waiting because fullness is still forming.

The iniquity of the Amorites is not yet full. (Genesis 15:16)

Fullness is not delay, it is evidence. When Scripture speaks of iniquity becoming "full," it is describing God completing the record. Fullness means that every restraint has been resisted, every warning has been ignored, and all opportunity for repentance has passed. Intent has been exposed; it is what it is.

At **fullness**, judgment is no longer debatable. Rescue is no longer questionable. Intervention is no longer premature. This is why God waits. Siege often exists because God is letting the record complete, all the while we may be asking the Lord, How long before you judge my enemies?

From inside a siege, it feels like abandonment. From heaven's perspective, it is documentation. Siege creates discomfort and pressure. Pressure reveals intent. What people do under pressure, how they act, how they speak, what they choose to do or not to do all becomes evidence. God does not need evidence for Himself. He allows it for righteousness' sake—so that when He acts, the matter is settled.

Power never leaves God's hands while He waits. Waiting is not weakness. Restraint is not absence. Silence is not surrender or abandonment.

God hath spoken once; twice have I heard this; that power belongeth unto God. (Psalm 62:11)

Scripture repeatedly warns us not to avenge ourselves. God will avenge all disobedience in our obedience. Do not force outcomes. Do not move without instruction and be anxious for nothing.

Besieged folks are called to remain obedient, even while under siege. Refuse compromise. do not negotiate with fear, or in fear. Do not abandon assignments. do not make permanent decisions under pressure.

The end is certain, but the timing is God's. Scripture never leaves siege unresolved. But it also never allows the besieged to dictate *how* or *when* resolution comes. Even if it is by God, through a Prophet, it is just that way. The prophet doesn't make up his own ting and make himself into a sub-God. (no such thing, really).

The way God ends it depends on the purpose of the siege and the outcome the Lord desires or the outcome He needs you to have which fit His plans and His plans for your life. Sometimes God prepares a table. Sometimes He commands threshing. Sometimes Historically, in the Bible He has sent one Angel, although He can send as many as He chooses. Sometimes He allows exile. He's God He knows best.

But always—power remains His.

God's delay is showing power under discipline. Fullness is not about time passing. It is about truth being exposed beyond appeal.

> I will never leave you nor forsake you.
> (Hebrews 13:5 (echoing Deuteronomy 31:6)

Siege does not mean abandonment. Waiting does not mean withdrawal. Silence does not mean absence. Encirclement does not mean ownership. God may restrain action, delay intervention, allow pressure, or permit fullness to form. But He never transfers covenant presence. Remember there are some things that cannot happen to you because of your Covenant with the Lord. There are things that the enemy can never do to you, because of Covenant.

A siege may remove every visible support, but it never removes God's covenant presence. He does not forsake His own—not in waiting, not in pressure, not in silence.

God does not forsake His own. Siege does not change that.

If you can understand the dynamics and the technology of breaking a personal siege, consider what your promotion may be. Now you can stand while God breaks a family siege, generational sieges, a bloodline siege, a siege over a territory or community. This is what the warnings have been about trying to engage territorial *spirits* and principalities. God does it, although He may have a man standing in the gap, in agreement.

Historically, if you look at whole cultures and people groups who seem to always be going through--- are they striving instead of letting go and letting God? Have they not put their entire trust in the Lord instead of leaning on their own understanding or man-made rituals (such as witchcraft just to endure or make it through, or relieve the symptoms further indebting their next generations? Pay attention here. Please.

The table has always been more than a place of comfort. In Scripture, the altar, the threshing floor, and the table are not separate ideas; they are stages of the same work. At the altar, something is offered. At the threshing floor, wheat is separated from the chaff. Jesus invited His Disciples to a table that came after pressure, after betrayal, after sifting had already begun.

So, when Jesus prepares a table, He is not pretending the siege never happened. He is declaring that the work is finished.

Was it not Jesus who fully *entered* the siege? Was it not Jesus who descended before He ascended? Promotion comes from the Lord. When you see what awaits you after outwaiting the siege, in the arms of the Lord, you will be sober, amazed, and thankful. Not only that, you will be ready for your next season and your next work in the Lord.

CONCLUSION

Humans don't break sieges; God does. And HE will COME.

If you have read this book slowly, some important things have already happened. You stopped blaming yourself. You did the work once you became aware that there were spiritual interferences. You did the praying, the studying, the praise and the worshiping, the fasting. You stopped trying to explain everything, as if there are words to explain anyway. You stopped assuming that pressure meant failure.

The siege is personal, but first you had to discern the source of it, if it is God, you go through the process. If it is not God, then there are different steps to take.

With God, a siege has a positive purpose, although it may feel negative. It's usually not comfortable until you realize that God is *all up in it.*

Without God, the enemy may only plan to box you in, corner you until you miss divine appointments or opportunities – or even miss destiny completely. He will try to use siege to steal, kill, and destroy; after all, that is his playbook. Without Divine Intervention from the Lord that could happen or even worse-- lights out.

But when you lean on God completely. When you put your trust and your faith in Him, even in the hard times, even in seemingly impossible times; He will deliver. And Amen to that.

A siege is containment with purpose. It is restraint that protects something too costly to rush, too fragile to expose, or too consequential to be shaped by desperation.

The pressure was real. The exhaustion was real. The temptation to self-solve was real. But the enemy believes the siege was to erase you, but with God, the script gets flipped and **you** are preserved while the one who wanted to erase you, goes *Bye Bye.*

The process and the victory of the siege is to promote. Was Job surrounded on all sides? Were things not working for him? Was everything he had been doing that used to work—did it stop working? Yes, to all those questions. Was Job then promoted and rewarded after all that? Yes, he was.

You were not asked to be stronger than human. You were not meant to endure by grit. You were not meant to win by force. You were not meant to out-pray, out-fast, or out-suffer the season. You were meant to remain governed. To wait without withering. To refuse self-rescue.. To resist being toyed with. To let authority return quietly, not theatrically. That is not weakness. That is maturity.

Self-rescue is **not** the answer to a siege, and now you know that. Desperation no longer governs you. Authority is being restored without damage. Complete relief comes from outside this season; it comes from the Lord.

When siege is over, you are not returning to who you were before. You are stepping forward as someone tempered, not diminished. You are better than you were when you leaned on the Lord and touched the Divine, because the Divine also touched you.

There is a new Glory, a different kind of Glory, a different kind of Light on someone who has been with the Lord, or in the Presence of the Lord. You are now that person. If it was your whole city – you are now that city.

This knowledge, this experience is not just for you, and it is not just for now. It is for every season that will come after this one. A siege ends. Always. Sometimes suddenly, sometimes quietly, sometimes without explanation. But when it ends, it does not leave you empty. It leaves you **established**.

Father God,
I release the need to rush what You are completing.
I receive the authority You have preserved.
I move forward without haste and without fear.

I am not desperate.
I am not prey.
I am not abandoned. I am established, in You.

In the Name of Jesus. **Amen.**

Dear Reader

Thank you for acquiring and reading this book, Seasons of Siege: God Is Coming. If you are the person who feels (or knows) that you are under siege, I pray this has increased your understanding of siege, it's reason for being, it's purposes and how to conduct yourself within it. I pray this book has set a path for God to help you, bless you, teach you, remove both your enemies and lift the siege. I pray that you will be closer to the Lord after this, established and even promoted. Under siege is serious and coming out of it is quite a blessing and an accomplishment.

Shalom,

Dr. Marlene Miles

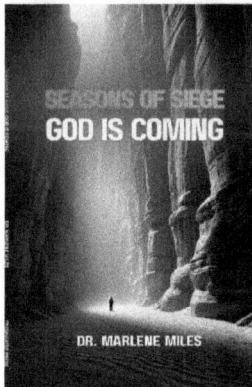

Prayerbooks by this author

There are some books that are only prayers. You just open up the book and pray.

Prayers Against Barrenness: *For Success in Business and Life*

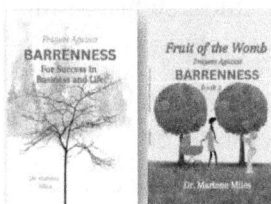

Fruit of the Womb: *Prayers Against Barrenness*

Beauty Curses, *Warfare Prayers Against*
https://a.co/d/5Xlc20M

Courts of Marriage: Prayers for Marriage in the Courts of Heaven *(prayerbook)* https://a.co/d/cNAdgAq

Courtroom Warfare @ Midnight *(prayerbook)*
https://a.co/d/5fc7Qdp

Demonic Cobwebs *(prayerbook)* https://a.co/d/fp9Oa2H

Every Evil Bird https://a.co/d/hF1kh1O

Gates of Thanksgiving

Spirits of Death, Hell & the Grave, Pass Over Me and My House

Throne of Grace: Courtroom Prayer

Warfare Prayer Against Poverty
https://a.co/d/bZ611Yu

Prayer Books by this Author

Prayer Manuals

FAKE FRIENDS: *Prayers Against Betrayers*

HOLIDAY WARFARE Prayer Manual (humorous) Surviving Family Gatherings All Year Long (without catching a case)

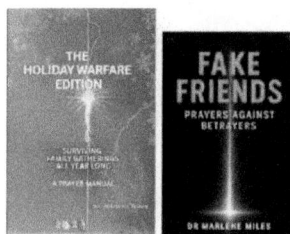

SOUL TIE Prayer Manual (The)   Part of a 3-part series including a workbook.

MAD at DADDY Prayer Manual – part of a 3-part series including a workbook.

Healing the Sibling & Relative Wound Prayer Manual

Healing the Father-Son Wound Prayer Manual

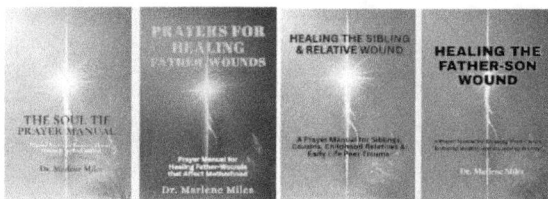

Prayers Against Barrenness: *For Success in Business and Life*

Breaking Curses of the Mother Prayer Manual

Other books by this author

Abundance of Jesus (The) https://a.co/d/5gHJVed

AK: The Adventures of the Agape Kid

Already Married in the Spirit: *Why You May Not Be Married in the Natural*

AMONG SOME THIEVES https://a.co/d/dkYT4ZV

Ancestral Powers

Anti-Marriage, *The Spirit of*

Backstabbers https://a.co/d/gi8iBxf

Barrenness, *Prayers Against* https://a.co/d/feUltIs

Battlefield of Marriage, *The*

Beware of the Dog: Prayers Against Dogs in the Dream.

Bless Your Food: *Let the Dining Table be Undefiled*
https://a.co/d/6oPMRDv

Blindsided: *Has the Old Man Bewitched You?*
https://a.co/d/5O2fLLR

Break Free from Collective Captivity

Broken Spirits & Dry Bones

By Means of a Whorish Father

Caged Life: Get Out Alive! https://a.co/d/bwPbksX

Casting Down Imaginations

Christ of God (The) 3-book series

Christ of God, Box Set, includes all three books

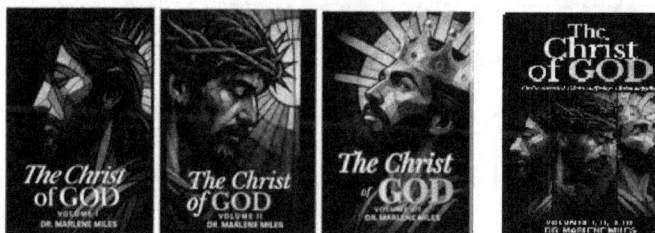

Churchzilla, The Wanna-Be, Supposed-to-be Bride of
Christ https://a.co/d/eAf5j3x

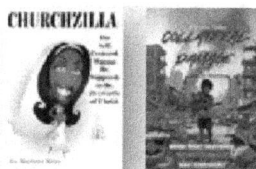

Collateral Damage: *When What Happened Spiritually Was Your Fault*

Demonic Cobwebs (prayerbook)

Demonic Time Bombs

Demons Hate Questions

Devil Loves Trauma, *The*

Devil Weapons: Unforgiveness, Bitterness,…

The Devourers: Thieves of Darkness 2

Do Not Swear by the Moon

Don't Refuse Me, Lord (4 book series)
https://a.co/d/idP34LG

Dream Defilement

The Emptiers: *Thieves of Darkness, 1*
https://a.co/d/5I4n5mc

Evil Touch

Failed Assignment

Fantasy Spirit Spouse https://a.co/d/hW7oYbX

FAT Demons (The): *Breaking Demonic Curses*
https://a.co/d/4kP8wV1

The Fold (5-book series)

- The Fold (Book 1)
- Name Your Seed (Book 2)
- The Poor Attitudes of Money (3)
- Do Not Orphan Your Seed (4)
- For the Sake of the Gospel (5)
- My Sowing Journal

Gang Ups: Touch Not God's Anointed

Gathered: No Longer Scattered
https://a.co/d/1i5DPIX

Getting Rid of Evil Spiritual Food

https://a.co/d/i2L3WYQ

got HEALING? Verses for Life

got LOVE? Verses for Life https://a.co/d/8seXHPd

got HOPE? Verses for Life

got money? https://a.co/d/g2av41N

Has My Soul Been Sold? https://a.co/d/dyB8hhA

Here Come the Horns: *Skilled to Destroy*
https://a.co/d/cZiNnkP

Hidden Sins: Hidden Iniquity

https://a.co/d/4MthOwa

How to Dental Assist

How to Dental Assist2: Be Productive, Not Wasteful

How to STOP Being a Blind Witch or Warlock

I Take It Back

Irresistible: Jesus' Triumphal Entry
https://a.co/d/dO9IfEC

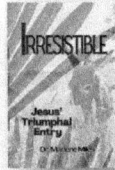

Legacy

Let Me Have A Dollar's Worth
https://a.co/d/h8F8XgE

Level the Playing Field

Living for the NOW of God

Lose My Location https://a.co/d/crD6mV9

Love Breaks Your Heart

Mad At Daddy: Healing Father-Wounds that Affect Motherhood (book, workbook & prayer manual)

Made Perfect In Love

Mammon https://a.co/d/29yhMG7

Man Safari, *The*

Marriage Ed. Rules of Engagement & Marriage

Made Perfect in Love

Money Hunters: Beware of Those

Money on the Altar https://a.co/d/4EqJ2Nr

Mulberry Tree, *The* https://a.co/d/9nR9rRb

Motherboard (The)- *Soul Prosperity Series*

Name Your Seed

Occupy: *Until I Return* https://a.co/d/bZ7ztUy

Opponent, Adversary, or Enemy?: Fight The Right Battle with the Right Weapons

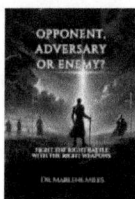

Plantation Souls

Players Gonna Play

Portals: Shut the Front Door: Prayers to Close Evil Portals.

Power Money: Nine Times the Tithe

https://a.co/d/gRt41gy

The Power to Get Wealth https://a.co/d/e4ub4Ov

Powers Above

The Robe, Part 1, The Lessons of Joseph

The Robe, Part II, The Lessons of Joseph

Seasons of Grief

Seasons of Siege

Seasons of Waiting

Seasons of War

Second Marriage, Third~~, *Any Marriage*

https://a.co/d/6m6GN4N

Seducing Spirits: Idolatry & Whoredoms

https://a.co/d/4Jq4WEs

Shut the Front Door: *Prayers to Close Portals*
https://a.co/d/cH4TWJj

Sift You Like Wheat

Six Men Short: What Has Happened to all the Men?

SLAVE

Sleep Afflictions & Really Bad Dreams
https://a.co/d/f8sDmgv

Soul Prosperity soul prosperity series 3

https://a.co/d/5p8YvCN

Soul Ties: How Soul Ties Form, and How To Break Them (book, workbook & prayer manual)

Souls Captivity soul prosperity series 2

The Spirit of Anti-Marriage

The Spirit of Poverty https://a.co/d/abV2o2e

Spiritual Thieves https://a.co/d/eqPPz33

StarStruck- Triangular Power series.

SUNBLOCK- Triangular Power series.

The Swallowers: *Thieves of Darkness*, 3

Take It Back

This Is NOT That: How to Keep Demons from Coming at You

Time Is of the Essence

Too Many Wives: *Why You Have Lady Problems*

Tormenting Spirits   https://a.co/d/dAogEJf

Toxic Souls

Triangular Power *(series),* Powers Above, SUNBLOCK, Do Not Swear by the Moon, STARSTRUCK

Unbreak My Heart: *Don't Let Me Die*

Uncontested Doom

Unguarded Hours, *The*

Unseen Life, *The* (forthcoming)

Upgrade: How to Get Out of Survival Mode Toxic Souls (Book 2 of series) , Legacy (Book 3 of series)

The Wasters: *Thieves of Darkness*, Bk 2
https://a.co/d/bUvI9Jo

What Have You to Declare? What Do You Have With You from Where You've Been?

When I Was A Child, *I Prayed As a Child*

When the Devourer is Rebuked

https://a.co/d/1HVv8oq

WTH? Get Me Out of This Hell
https://a.co/d/a7WBGJh

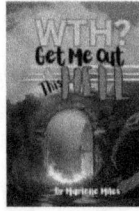

The Wilderness Romance *(series)* This series is about conducting a Godly relationship and marriage with someone who is a Wilderness person. It is about how to recognize it and navigate through it. These books are about how not to get caught up in such.

- *The Social Wilderness*
- *The Sexual Wilderness*
- *The Spiritual Wilderness*

Other Series

The Fold (a series on Godly finances) https://a.co/d/4hz3unj

Soul Prosperity Series https://a.co/d/bz2M42q

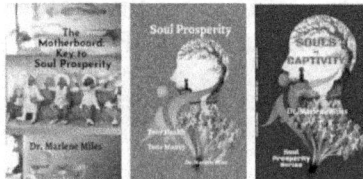

Spirit Spouse books

https://a.co/d/9VehDSo

https://a.co/d/97sKOwm

Battlefield of Marriage, The

https://a.co/d/eUDzizO

Players Gonna Play

https://a.co/d/2hzGw3N

Sent Spirit Spouse (can someone send you a spirit spouse? This book is not yet released.)

Matters of the Heart, Made Perfect in Love
https://a.co/d/70MQW3O , Love Breaks Your Heart https://a.co/d/4KvuQLZ, Unbreak My Heart https://a.co/d/84ceZ6M Broken Spirits & Dry Bones https://a.co/d/e6iedNP

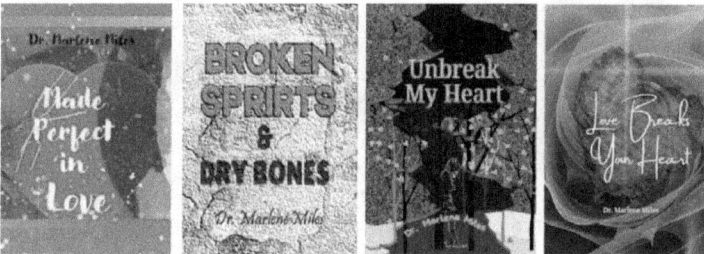

Thieves of Darkness series

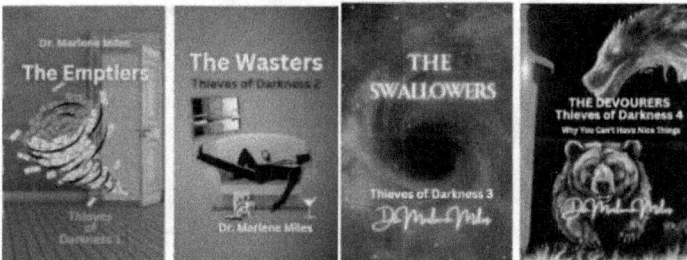

The Emptiers https://a.co/d/heio0dO

The Wasters https://a.co/d/5TG1iNQ

The Swallowers https://a.co/d/1jWhM6G

The Devourers: Why We Can't Have Nice Things https://a.co/d/87Tejbf

Spiritual Thieves

Triangular Powers https://a.co/d/aUCjAWC

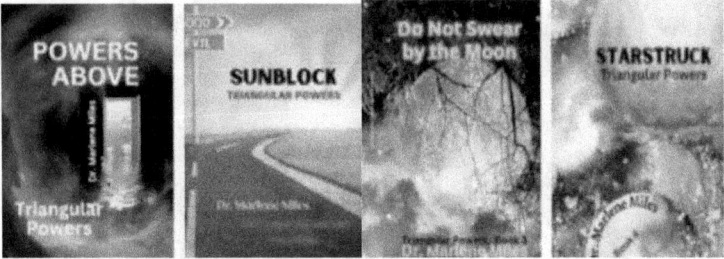

Upgrade (series) *How to Get Out of Survival Mode*
https://a.co/d/aTERhX0

We Get Along, Right? Compatibility for Couples – (book & workbook)

www.ingramcontent.com/pod-product-compliance
Lightning Source LLC
LaVergne TN
LVHW052028080426
835513LV00018B/2227